WARTIME KENT 1939-40

A Selection of Memories from the BBC Radio Kent Series

Compiled by
OONAGH HYNDMAN

MERESBOROUGH BOOKS

Published by Meresborough Books, 17 Station Road, Rainham, Kent, ME8 7RS in association with BBC Radio Kent.

Meresborough Books is a specialist publisher of books about Kent. A list of titles currently available will be sent on request. A few are listed on the back page.

Also published in association with BBC Radio Kent:
The Radio Kent Gardeners' Guide by Harry Smith and Bob Collard. £3.95 (£4.35 by post).

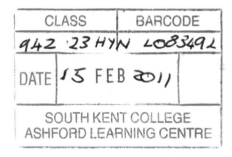

ISBN 0948193 611

Printed and bound in Great Britain by
Biddles Ltd, Guildford and King's Lynn

CONTENTS

FOREWORD

It's two years since I arrived at Sun Pier, sure in my mind of at least one thing — that listeners to BBC Radio Kent would expect the 50th anniversary of World War 2 to be commemorated on the air.

Those memories would be too deep, too vivid, too intense to be ignored by a community-based radio station.

What that meant in practical terms was detailing some of our scarce resources towards research and preparation for programmes. But one other thing I was sure of was that our listeners would, as ever, respond to an appeal for help.

I had one other conviction — that the resulting programmes should not just convey the excitement of a teenager given a Spitfire to fly, the sorrow of a war widow, the fear of bombing, the closeness of relationships. They should also be a lesson to younger people, to those who had not experienced those years personally, that war is evil.

In the event the programmes have been superb — a credit to the production team, in the true BBC tradition. Above all a tribute to all our listeners who responded with their stories and a memorial to all those who died.

That is not me talking, that is the message which has come by letter, by phone call and in conversation from you, our listeners, and it is you we have to thank.

I hope this book, a record of your stories, keeps those memories alive.

Jim Latham
Managing Editor
BBC Radio Kent

INTRODUCTION

This book is not intended to be a definitive history of World War II as experienced by those who lived in the County of Kent. The aim is to commit to the printed word the wartime recollections of those who chose to share their memories of the early war years with BBC Radio Kent's listeners.

In April 1989 the first of a series of documentary programmes was broadcast recalling the mundane and the dramatic occurrences of the Second World War as remembered by our contributors. The result of that programme, and those which followed, was an ever-snowballing avalanche of letters, the majority of which were followed up by interview. The story which unfolds is ultimately a team effort — the First Team being our respondents, who remember with chuckles and tears the way life was. The Second Team is the Radio Kent trio who have criss-crossed the county in search of stories. Producers Helen Mayhew and Honor Morris and Programme Researcher Sally Kimber, with a special mention for the sound engineers who helped an electronically ignorant author gather the material. Inevitably some memories have been omitted and I apologise to those people but hope that in sharing this story of Wartime Kent, their disappointment will be lessened.

Oonagh Hyndman

ACKNOWLEDGEMENTS

My thanks go to Radio Kent listeners whose memories I have read and listened to with pleasure and who have entrusted us with their memorabilia and photographs. Many museum curators, librarians and individuals have given generously of their time and knowledge. My thanks go to the Imperial War Museum Sound Archives, to Tom White, curator of Kent Fire Brigade Museum, and Arnold Saddleton, Kent Fire Brigade photographer. Librarians at Dover, Canterbury, Coxheath, Maidstone Reference Section and Springfield have been most helpful. A particular thank you must go to the Kent History Centre at Cornwallis School Linton, where Ian Coulson has a rich collection of material. Robin Brooks and Ted Sergison of The Kent Aviation Historical Research Society always made themselves available to help with finer points of technical interpretation. I am especially grateful to my family who throughout the long hot summer of 1990 listened to wartime memories and helped identify occasional difficult phrases such as 'Fifth Columnists' and 'Water Boatmen'. Finally, my profound thanks to my daughter-in-law Vivienne Hyndman for her indomitable cheerfulness while typing this manuscript.

Oonagh Hyndman

WARTIME KENT CONTRIBUTORS

Biddy Allen	Dick Body	Mary Chantler
Ronald Allen	Frank Bond	Joan Chinery
Alison Ashford	Peter Boulden	Joan Clark
Doris Ayres	Doreen Bradley	Percy Clarke
Winifred Baker	Robin Brooks	Margaret Collins
Paddy Barthropp	Jack Browning	Beryl Cooper
Dorothy Barton	Stanley Caleno	Freddie Cooper
Roger Bellamy	Bill Callan	Jimmy Corbin
Walter Bevan	Michael Calvert	Don Crisp
Joyce Bishop	Mary Cannon	Evelyn Cundy
Jeanne Blackmore	Ron Cattell	John Curley
Arthur Blow	George Cawte	Colin Cuthbert
Lilian Blow	Reg Chambers	Reg Cutting

George Darley
Stanley Day
Gwen Devereux
Joan Disney
Blanche Donovan
Nora Doughty
Martyn Down
Fred Dunston
Eileen Dykes
Wilfred Dykes
Harry Eede
Claud Evernden
Josie Fairclough
Gordon Farrer
Daphne Faulder
Vera Ferris
Michael Fitzgerald
Philip Franks
George Freeland
Eddie Fryer
Chrissie Gallivan
Ken Geering
Joyce Gilham
Tom Gleave
Fred Gore
Vicki Graham
Charles Griffin
Fred Hadlow
Ursula Hall-Thompson
Betty Harden
Norman Hayes
William Hewitt
Mary Hilliker
Marion Hinkley
Vera Holdstock
Alex Howard
Frank Howard

Olive Howard
John Howarth
Rosemary Huckerby
Joan Ingram
Cyril Innis
Peggy Jenkins
Ted Jenkins
Mabel Jenner
Mick Johns
Brenda Keatley
George Kellett
Albert Kidgell
Bob Layton
Doug Lee
Barbara Letchford
Bert Lewis
Fred Lewis
Gwen Lonsdale
Betty Marden
Arthur Marsh
Lena Marshall
Beryl Mason
Martin Mason
Peter Matthews
Margaret McIntyre
Ron Mercer
Tom Miller
Ian Moat
Beryl Moore
Lilian Morris
Bessie Newton
Mary O'Connolly
Leslie Page
Lilian Parkes
Eric Pearson
Eric Pemberton
Harry Pickett

Joyce Rayner
Joan Rootes
Dick Rose
Jack Sharp
Joan Small
Arthur Smith
Leonard Smith
Mary Smith
Olive Solomon
George Sone
Rene Spellward
Laurie Springett
Bobbie Stacey
Frank Stanford
Norman Steed
Ulrich Steinhilper
Jim Stokes
Mary Sullivan
Winifred Swain
Catherine Taylor
Dolly Taylor
Johnny Thompson
Geoff Tinley
Vi Tippett
Gladys Townshend
John Ullman
Bob Viney
Stan Walton
Bunny Wareham
Norman Webber
Charlie Wheeler
Dick Whittamore
Mary Wickham
Gladys Wilber
Evelyn Wilson
Ruth Wilson
Ernie Wood

PUBLIC NOTICE

NOTICE

KENT COUNTY COUNCIL

AIR RAID PRECAUTIONS

Defence Exercise 9th/10th August, 1939

A BLACK-OUT WILL BE ARRANGED as follows:—

All County Districts excluding those comprised within the Metropolitan Police District — From 12 midnight 9th August, 1939 To 4.0 a.m. 10th August, 1939

All County Districts comprised within the Metropolitan Police District — From 12.30 a.m. 10th August, 1939 To 4.0 a.m. 10th August, 1939

It is desired to secure that no lights are visible from the air during the period of the Black-out. The darkening of areas exposed to air attack may be expected to be an essential feature of the defence of this country in time of war, and useful information on the best means of effecting this may be derived from the present Exercise.

HOUSEHOLDERS AND ALL OTHER OCCUPIERS OF PREMISES ARE ACCORDINGLY ASKED TO ASSIST BY ENSURING THAT LIGHTS IN THEIR PREMISES ARE EXTINGUISHED, OR SCREENED BY DARK CURTAIN OR BLINDS, DURING THE PERIOD OF THE BLACK-OUT. IT IS PARTICULARLY DESIRABLE THAT EXTERNAL LIGHTS AND OTHER LIGHTS DIRECTLY VISIBLE FROM THE SKY SHOULD BE EXTINGUISHED OR SCREENED.

As lighting in streets will be restricted, vehicles should, so far as possible, keep off the roads during the darkened period.

It is emphasised that there is no intention, in connection with the Black-out, of cutting off lighting or power supplies at the mains.

NOTE.—If owing to weather conditions it is necessary to postpone the Black-out, an announcement will be made by the British Broadcasting Corporation in the 6.0 p.m. news bulletin on the 9th August, 1939. Great care should be exercised, therefore, to ensure that all necessary precautions are taken to secure a complete Black-out on the date finally determined.

Public Notice from 'The Kentish Express', 4th August 1939.   (Kent History Centre)

Chapter I
THE COUNTRY PREPARES

Preparations for war in the county of Kent as we know it today were under the overall control of Sir Auckland Geddes, the South East Regional Commissioner for Civil Defence organised from his headquarters at Mount Ephraim, Tunbridge Wells. The country had been divided into twelve regions and the Kent boroughs to the north of the county were within the jurisdiction of the London region. Civil defence was administered by committee who for months, and indeed in some cases years before the oubreak of war, addressed the particular problems which could face the county. Geographically vulnerable to air attack being between the Continent and London, the authorities had also to consider the defence of Kent's long coastline.

Air raid warning systems, simulated gas attacks, the establishment of telephone communications and organising the blackout as well as deciding which towns in Kent would be safe areas to receive evacuees, occupied considerable administrative time.

The Royal Air Force paid close attention to the aerodromes in the county but it was not only the military airfields which were prepared for war as Robin Brooks from Maidstone explains:

'All the aerodromes were grass at that time and the runways were strengthened with a type of planking called Sommerfeld Tracking. This was laid on the grass to give it a good surface for aircraft to land on and take off. Apart from grass runways, the airfields had hangarage for aircraft. Some of the men's accommodation was in tents but some of the airfields also had brick buildings. During 1938 as the threat from Germany grew closer and closer, many of the flying clubs had to accept personnel under training who were in the civil air guard which was really a military back-up of pilots. During 1938 and 1939, aircraft were put on to a wartime footing hastily camouflaged, with colourful squadron markings a thing of the past. During this growth period it seemed as if Kent was swamped in airfields but, as we had the closest coastline to Germany, it was obvious the onslaught would come across the channel.'

The railway lines in the county required protection and Dick Rose of Folkestone, a sub-ganger working for Southern Railway, describes the secret plan in action:

'I had in my possession for some time, a properly sealed envelope marked, "Most Secret, only to be opened by instructions when war is imminent." On Friday 1st September 1939 at 1600 hours I received a telephone call from the engineer telling me plainly to open that letter. It said we should start night patrols immediately with four patrolmen on the sixteen miles of track.

'The patrolmen were to report to me about every hour throughout the night to make sure all was well. They were very concerned in those days about fifth column activities and they did not know whether the bombs were going to be put under bridges or on the track or what was to happen. The patrol was on the track between Cheriton junction as far as Harbledown junction which is in Canterbury.'

Walter Bevan describes the war-time preparations in Longfield:

'The Home Guard did not come until later but then they had the national fire service civil defence parties, first aid parties. The local council depot was turned into what they called "heavy rescue" which meant they had the equipment to dig people out of bombed houses, there were leaflets distributed everywhere and we were fitted out with gas masks and eventually issued with air raid shelters. There were boards put around the village which had special paint on which reacted to mustard gas and then we had instructions telling us that the church bells would mean invasion, rattles would mean gas, long blasts on the whistle by the air raid warden was the all clear and short sharp blasts meant the alert. So the village gathered itself to war.'

Geoff Tinley was a schoolboy living in Buckland near Dover when war was declared. He remembers what life was like growing up in a small village:

'Not a lot of travelling about by car. If you weren't a doctor you didn't have one. Things were still delivered to the door in the old-fashioned way. The milkman would ladle milk out by the pint. People didn't move very far from the area and consequently, you knew your home town very well indeed.'

Just before the war broke out, and indeed in the early part of the war, a few less public-spirited people bought in extra supplies of food to tide them over in anticipation of rationing, but the option of hoarding was not available to most people as Dick Whittamore from Dover explains:

'In those days we were so poor ourselves and I think most people seemed to be poor, they wouldn't have had the money. I can remember the price of sugar jumping up just after the war broke out. It seemed to be tuppence (1p) a pound one week and the next week you went and bought it, it was eight pence (3½p) per pound.'

During the Munich crisis in 1938 trenches had been dug and gas masks issued. However, there was an air of unreality about life and whatever the official preparation, many private people almost ignored what was happening.

Vi Tippett from Rainham who ran a boarding house in Margate remembers:

'We'd got our gas masks, those awful things in boxes, apart from that I don't think there was any preparation. Some people had stocked their cupboards but not everybody. It was a half-hearted affair. Although we were all frightened, I don't think anybody thought it would come to that. Mr Chamberlain was going to save us, people said if the worst comes it will be over by Christmas.'

Gas masks were seen as theatening by many people, including Geoff Tinley who celebrated his tenth birthday the day before war was declared and who remembers:

'My father and mother had both gone through the First World War, though neither of them were old enough to serve in it. I can remember my father telling me about Zeppelin raids, but they didn't mean much to a ten-year-old boy, who certainly lived in a world of his own. They were all just exciting stories. I think what bothered people most was having been issued with gas masks, the thought of a gas attack really brought terror to most people's hearts, especially youngsters, because it was something we couldn't understand.'

Lilian Morris of Dartford was living in Bredhurst, her husband already posted to the Middle East with the Royal Corps of Signals. Her first baby, a son, was born seven months after he sailed and because letters were delayed he only heard the news just before the birth.

'I was so thrilled to have the baby but very very worried, especially when they talked about gas masks and I used to think "What's it going to be like fitting a gas mask on a baby?" and I was praying that I would never have to use one.'

Lilian's fears were shared at the same time by Winifred Swain who was living in Canterbury. Her daughter was just two years old.

'My first thoughts were I'd got a gas mask and my little girl hadn't. I said "Why ever did we have her if she's going to have to face all this?" I remember getting into a terrible state over it.'

Children and babies were issued with special masks. The Mickey Mouse mask, so called because it resembled the face of the popular cartoon character, was painted blue and red and was meant to be worn by very young children. Some quite enjoyed wearing it, you could apparently blow very effective raspberries through it, but others still found the mask frightening as Margaret McIntyre from Sutton Valence describes:

'My sister was only five so she had a Mickey Mouse one. I remember that clearly, she hated it and when we were at school and had to practise putting it on, she used to cry.'

HAVE YOU ADEQUATE SHELTER AGAINST AIR RAIDS?

You are entitled to EXPERT ADVICE and FREE ASSISTANCE* regarding the preparation of a

REFUGE ROOM or SHELTER
in your own home.

With the approach of fine weather, increasingly severe air attacks are likely to be experienced.

A high degree of safety and convenience can be secured by house adaptation in accordance with certain technically recognised standards, and the Local Authority will give assistance in carrying out the necessary work FREE OR AT COST, according to certain income limits (stated below).

IF YOU HAVE NO SHELTER OF ANY KIND, YOU ARE STRONGLY URGED IN YOUR OWN INTERESTS AND FOR THE SAFETY OF MEMBERS OF YOUR HOUSEHOLD TO AVAIL YOURSELF OF THIS OFFER.

DON'T DELAY
Send a postcard or register your name & address at the A.R.P. Offices, 43 Queen Street, Deal. Arrangements will then be made for a representative to call on you.

* Note.—If your income is £350 per annum or less you are entitled to free assistance and materials. Certain allowances above this limit are made for children beyond the first two.

Leaflet issued by the Civil Defence Services of the Borough of Deal.   (Kent History Centre)

Jack Browning's behaviour did nothing whatever to alleviate such fears. He recalls making mischief in Ramsgate:

'When we were at school around 1938, I got my first gas mask. I was about to leave school then, which I did. I put this gas mask on thinking something's going to happen, I was only a young lad then and I was trying to frighten the young children in the junior school with it.'

Daphne Faulder from Lenham was a twelve-year-old pupil at East Borough in Maidstone but for her it was not the colour or the shape of the mask which mattered:

'They smelt very rubbery, the smell of rubber always brings back the memories of the gas mask.'

The government issued a special book for animals in 1939, stating that they would be banned from air raid shelters. Gas masks for animals would be of no use, the booklet warned, as a masked animal would lose its sense of smell.

In the days when war was imminent, people prepared for the worst. For those who were expecting to be evacuated from danger areas, provision for their pet animals had to be made. Vi Tippett:

'We had to queue to have our animals put to sleep which was bad, but they told us that if we had to go away and leave them they would starve and the kindest thing was to do that.'

In those early days it was an airborne gas attack, rather than bombs, which people feared. An official government poster issued at the outbreak of the war in 1939 read: 'Hitler will give no warning . . . always carry your gas masks'.

It was an all too real threat. Poison gas, particularly the dreaded mustard gas which had been used on soldiers in the trenches at the end of the First World War, had an horrific effect. Many died and those who did not often endured terrible suffering for the rest of their lives. It was a punishable offence to be seen without a gas mask and there was a rush on supplies at the beginning of the war.

Ruth Wilson of Dover worked for the local council in Faversham at the time:

'We had to go to a large hall many of us and help to make gas masks. My word that was hard on the fingers.'

The gas masks were reputed to cost half a crown each to manufacture and were intended to be easy and quick to fit. The idea was to thrust your chin into the mask and pull it over your face and head, securing it at the back with three straps. The civilian type respirator, to give it the official name, had a small filter and transparent panel over the eyes. A special military-type mask was issued to people whom it was thought were likely to experience a heavy concentration of gas.

People like Brenda Keatley's father, who was a signalman at Ramsgate Station. Brenda remembers how his mask appeared to her, a nine-year-old:

'Dad had a great big one, it was like a great big piggy, I suppose it lasted longer, but the servicemen had bigger ones anyway. He looked just like a pig in it.'

Gas masks had to be taken everywhere with you as Beryl Moore from Sutton Valence recalls. She was fourteen years old and living with her widowed mother in Gillingham when the war started:

'Everyone prayed that we'd never have to use our gas masks. We'd been issued with them at the beginning and as you went out the door, everyone called out, "Got your gas mask?"'

Frank Stanford of Sevenoaks, a twelve-year-old living in St Margaret's Bay, agrees with Beryl:

'That's the only thing that everybody knew during the war, you took it everywhere even to the toilet, even took it to bed, that box with the gas mask in.'

Brenda Keatley from Ramsgate was another dutiful child:

'You always had your gas mask with you, like your identity card that went everywhere with you too. The mask was in a cardboard box to start with and later you could have a proper case.'

Joan Disney from Longfield, a wartime schoolgirl, remembers the burden of her gas mask and her iron rations:

'We used to have a two mile walk to school, come home at lunch time because there were no school dinners, so most of my day was spent walking back and forwards to school. We used to have our gas masks and a tin with iron rations. When I say iron, they were hard biscuits, harder than cream crackers, a piece of cheese and a piece of chocolate and it was with great difficulty that the chocolate stayed in our ration boxes. We used to have an inspection two or three times a week at school to make sure we'd got our gas masks and our rations.'

The tops of pillar boxes in the towns and what was then called 'Street Furniture', were painted yellow with sensitive paint which would change colour to reveal the first drops of the dreaded mustard gas. The government also urged people to gas proof their homes by using pulped paper to seal up the cracks round windows. Local newspapers gave detailed instructions as to what people should do, as Winifred Swain recalls:

'We sealed a little bedroom for our daughter and tried to make it gas proof, which they advised us to do. We really thought she was going to be gassed.'

The blackout was another wartime restriction which affected everyone. The scheme required all lights to be covered up after dark, to protect inhabited areas from the threat of night-time bombing raids. In the month leading up to the out-break of war, the government mounted a campaign to make everyone aware of the need for lights to be masked at night-time, should war be declared.

In July 1939 a leaflet with the unimaginative title of 'Public Information Leaflet No.2' was delivered to every household, giving detailed information on how to make doors and windows light proof. Many optimists who thought the war would be over by Christmas made temporary blinds out of paper, but these tore easily and they were soon discarded for a more permanent version.

Prior to the outbreak of war the government had arranged for shops to have stocks of blackout material available, but the supply was often outstripped by demand, forcing many to improvise.

Joyce Gilham's brother made shutters from wood and roof felt for their Kemsley home — all in one day. While Mary Chantler, then a nineteen-year-old newly-wed farmer's wife from Homestall Farm, Headcorn, experimented:

'It was a nightmare. We had to buy black material to cover the windows and because we weren't very well off we bought as little as we could and stretched it over the window which meant we had gaps each side and we were always being told off by the warden. Some people used to put blankets up but what they didn't think about were the holes in them, so of course they were told off by the warden. I thought I'd be clever and make a black lampshade which I very proudly showed everyone, but during the evening it caught alight and burnt out so we had to think again about that.'

Walter Bevan, a young man facing his last months at school, recalls some helpful measures which were taken to combat the blackout.

'The car bumpers were painted white so as to give a bit more light, then white lines were put on the road and on the kerbs to give you a guide.'

The blackout was very strictly enforced and many people were more afraid of being caught by the police or wardens for showing a light than they were of the Germans. A Ramsgate millionaire, Arthur Nash, became one of the first people in the country to be prosecuted for breaking the blackout laws, after an angry crowd had gathered outside his house to protest at his unscreened windows. He was fined a total of £15. For the people going about their business after dark the blackout was a real trial as Dick Whittamore remembers:

'You walked into lamp-posts mainly, on a very dark night you had to be careful of lamp-posts although if you used the same street night after night you knew exactly where they were so you could avoid them. If you didn't bump into lamp-posts you bumped into other people. I had a bicycle with a light on it and that was dipped towards the roadside all the time.'

If the owners of modest homes had trouble keeping the lights in, those with larger properties found the blackout even more of a nightmare due to the hours it took to put up and take down the blinds every day. Shops, pubs and factories

Kitted out to survive an attack of mustard gas.   (Kent History Centre)

had to be blacked out and even cars, trains and buses were subject to restrictions as Margaret Collins from Maidstone remembers:

'The blackout caused all kinds of problems, cars for instance had open little slits for headlights, in buses and in trains the windows were blacked out so you couldn't see out of them at all.'

Just one of those problems is explained by Dick Whittamore:

'One evening I was going down the street on my cycle and I heard an aeroplane above with a whistle telling me the bombs were coming. I just flung my bike in the middle of the road, dashed into a doorway and a lady walking down the road went straight into my bicycle. Funnily enough she wasn't concerned with the bombs, all she was concerned with was that she had laddered her stockings and you couldn't get them during the war.'

Ken Geering, an Ashford councillor representing North Ward, remembers walking down Ashford High Street:

'I was with my wife, she complained that she couldn't see and I said, "Look up my dear and you can see perfectly well," at which point I collided with a lamp-post, rather painful.'

Walter Bevan's uncle was another hapless casualty as Walter explains. 'He came out of our local public house, The Railway Tavern in Longfield, one night and he was a pipe smoker. He walked straight into a tree which rammed the stem of his pipe right down his throat and the bowl burnt his nose.'

People in Kent soon became accustomed to the necessity of providing a shelter for themselves or making themselves aware of the shelters which had been provided in the towns. The first and most common type of air raid shelter was the Anderson, named after the Home Secretary, Sir John Anderson. It was designed in 1938 by William Patterson, a Scottish engineer and was a cheap, effective domestic shelter. The Anderson was an arched shelter made of thick curved steel sheets which had to be erected in a hole of four feet deep, and then covered with the earth from the hole. The result was like a small underground bicycle shed with an entrance hole at ground level. Andersons were provided free to manual workers in danger areas and to others earning under £250 per year, or you could buy them for £7.

For those who could afford it, G.S. Joiner at Herne Bay, Builder and Contractor, advertised air raid and gas proof shelters, built to plans and specification approved by the Home Office. Suitable for six or seven persons, the shelters had solid reinforced concrete walls and came completed with a gas curtain at a price of £50; smaller shelters could be built at a reduced cost.

Dick Whittamore remembers the Dover shelters:

'In the cliffs beneath Dover, there have been caves for many years and, obviously, they were opened up for wartime use so that when the first sirens went, people rushed for them. They were very, very damp being chalk and they weren't very warm either. There were several in the town, especially in the seafront areas, including one underneath Woolworths. There were other basement shelters in the town with signs directing you to them. Air raid warnings were tested before the war to get people used to them, so we were prepared for war.'

There were many places in Kent which provided good, natural shelter besides the well known Dover caves and tunnels in Ramsgate. These included the Chislehurst Caves, tunnels under the Fort Gardens in Gravesend and various tunnels along the cliff face beside the Thames, from Gravesend to Greenhithe. There were also tunnels in the Medway towns as Evelyn Wilson, a ten-year-old at the time, recalls:

'We lived up on the Darland Banks in Chatham and there is a big fort up there. My cousin and I used to play in this fort pre-war. It was a big long tunnel with ante-rooms off it. When the sirens went in the war we used to go over there with our pouffes and blankets and sit down in this big fort.'

Jack Browning from Ramsgate remembers the re-opening of the Ramsgate tunnels. 'In 1938 Ramsgate had already dug out many tunnels for air raid shelters which led into a main tunnel. This had been Ramsgate Harbour Station, which closed in 1926.'

Fred Gore, who is still a Ramsgate resident, recalls:

'I myself sent out a plan to the ARP suggesting that the old railway tunnel built in 1825 could be connected with the town tunnels. This was done. You could walk from the old railway tunnel all around Ramsgate to the General Hospital where there was a tunnel where I think they had a type of surgery there for people who were injured.'

Vera Ferris, a Ramsgate teenager, describes the tunnels in the beginning:

'To start off with we had nothing, we used to take down deck-chairs and we used to sleep on them.'

Some people sensibly used their shelters from the very beginning of war as Alison Ashford from Bearsted remembers. Her family had recently returned from South Africa where her father had worked with medical missionaries at a leper hospital.

'I was just thirteen years old and my parents had a shelter built underground in our garden in Folkestone and in those first weeks I remember frantic sorties out to the shelter, sometimes in the dead of night.

'My father, who was a Minister, would always go first and he would lead Mother by the hand and we four children would follow. There were seats in the shelter and we would sit and try to sing. Of course, as you know, nothing happened, but there was the fright especially at night.'

Less obvious than the blackout preparations, gas mask and shelter provision were the plans to receive evacuees with some remarkably short distances envisaged as being safe as Dick Whittamore's memory illustrates:

'There had been a threat of war for some considerable time and during my last year at school I can remember the head teacher telling us that if war was declared quite a few children would be billeted out to the country. I lived in East Langdon about four or fives miles outside Dover. If the Germans bombarded Dover, we were to expect loads of children to come to our school from the town.'

Holidaymakers in Margate needed to distance themselves further than four or five miles from the Kent coast. They listened carefully to the wireless and on the last weekend of peace decided that whatever the attractions of the seaside, it was not a safe place to stay, as Gwen Devereux remembers:

'There were a lot of visitors here and they all vanished. I was working at a hotel here on Margate seafront and so was my husband and they fled back to their homes and we were out of a job. We cleaned up and that was it — there was no more.'

Vi Tippett shared that experience:

'My husband was working at the Home and Colonial and I kept a small boarding house. The summer was very busy because people did not go abroad in those days and Margate was a really nice place then. The day before war was declared, everybody went home. They were frightened, Margate was too near to France, they really were frightened.'

There were Germans and other aliens in the county before the war broke out and some took the decision to return to their homeland as tension in Europe grew. German teachers and students were resident in the county's schools, including the Maidstone Grammar School for Girls where they had a student teacher to give German lessons, as Doris Ayres remembers:

'Of course when the war broke out she had orders to disappear, but she hadn't got any money to get back to Germany so the staff had to contribute to her fare. Her favourite walk was up in the hills at Detling near the aerodrome.'

At the same time, Jewish refugees arrived in Kent in the months leading up to the outbreak of war to escape Nazi persecution and some were sheltered in a transit camp at Richborough near Sandwich.

The Richborough camp had been established during the First World War as a secret terminal for the movement of troops and ammunitions to France and Flanders. After the war it fell into disrepair but was re-opened in 1939 as a refuge for those fleeing from Germany, Austria and Czechoslovakia. The intention was that Richborough would be the first stage in evacuation to other countries and refugees had their passports stamped with permission indicating that they could proceed to be registered at Richborough. These permits were strictly limited by quota and the camp was regarded as a life saver by the refugees.

Most of the refugees arrived at Richborough after an exhausting and often frightening journey by train through Europe and by ferry to Dover. Having left friends, home and family behind, they faced an uncertain future in a strange land.

Lena Marshall, a twenty-year-old living near Manston, believed that there was no danger of another war until she saw the refugees arrive.

'I began to realise that something I had believed to be quite impossible was in fact possible. No one who met these men could be unaware of the hopeless bewilderment and horror that was shown on their faces and in their eyes.'

The Richborough camp occupied buildings on both sides of the Sandwich to Ramsgate road and the two sections were known as the Kitchener Camp and the Haig Camp. Phineas May, Temporary Quartermaster and Storekeeper of the Kitchener Camp, kept a diary between January and August 1939 which clearly indicates the effect of the camp on the economy of Sandwich. Contracts were negotiated for the supply of food and coal, and local women engaged as camp cleaners. Sandwich residents reciprocated by offering land at the disposal of the refugees so that they could train in agriculture, a hardware shop donated a dart board and the cinema manager allowed the refugees the best seats at the cut price of 6d (2½p).

19

Joan Disney walked eight miles to and from school — resisting the piece of chocolate in her tin of iron rations.

(J. Disney)

Life for the refugees was very different from the one they had left behind, especially for Bob Layton who weeks earlier had been in the Dachau concentration camp.

'The camp wasn't well organised at that time, I think the first people arrived about a month before, trades people. As I had been a motor engineer I was put in charge of transport with some very old fashioned vehicles which I had to look after.'

Bob was unexpectedly set free from Dachau in February 1939. The Nazi Authorities released him on the condition that he would be sent on to Shanghai in China as a refugee. His mother and sister arranged the papers necessary for him to be taken to the transit camp in Richborough. Bob describes his arrival:

'We arrived in Dover and had our first cup of tea with milk, and it was awful stuff, special station tea. It was dark and I didn't know it was Dover, I had no idea where we were but I soon found out when we got into the camp where we were given a meal late at night. My friend collected me in one of those big trucks. Not just me, there were hundreds of us, several hundred anyhow.

'We were taught how to behave and how to approach English people and were actually issued with a book to give us an idea how English people

20

behave. I enjoyed the freedom to speak to whom you want and say what you like, it was a marvellous feeling. It didn't matter what the conditions were like, it was completely unimportant because we were used to much more terrible conditions. We rebuilt the camp, put roads in and every time we finished a bit of road we put the white tape across and cut it. We had our own orchestra and a cinema and I think Lord Austen gave us a projector and a friend of mine, an electrician, wired it up and got it going so there was lovely entertainment. I had a garage by the small lake where we repaired all the vehicles. We kept terribly busy and worked very very hard to get this camp ready for other refugees to arrive at a later date.'

For some of the refugees the Richborough Camp was something of a disappointment, especially for Philip Franks from Berlin, a nineteen-year-old, who had come from a fairly comfortable background:

'You were safe, physically safe, but what the future was bringing with no money because all we were allowed to take was a suitcase and seventeen shillings (85p), so you were dependent on charity from other people. It was very difficult. We arrived late at night. It had been raining and as we jumped out of the bus I jumped straight into a puddle.

'We got into our hut and we had something to eat which was very good. It was primitive in lots of ways and we worked and repaired the huts which had been empty since the previous world war. It was like a ghost camp. We repaired all the huts so that other people could come over.'

Fred Dunston, a twenty-three-year-old from Vienna, had mixed feelings about being in Richborough:

'The German voices I had recently heard in Austria all belonged to Nazis so the first thing that hit me personally were the German accents and dialects in the camp where the majority of men were Germans. It took me more than a week to shake off that feeling of fear, that horrible fear that I was still surrounded by Nazis.

'The discipline was very strict, we were really behind barbed wire, that in a way was a bit of a shock. Once you are behind barbed wire, you are not free and you needed a permit which one could obtain, but not easily, to leave camp. Of course, the uncertainty as to how long one would have to stay at the camp and what would happen to one's relatives, I had all this on my mind.'

Having got through those difficult first days, Fred Dunston settled in to camp life:

'The Germans liked discipline but for us there was almost too much discipline. There was a regular timetable and I had to do one or two things, English lessons, which didn't worry me because I had quite a good knowledge from school and private lessons and then one had to choose a subject

21

like carpentry, agriculture training or whatever. The time was divided and there were games; I wasn't a very great sportsman, but there was time for sport and occasionally one could get a permit and have a chance to get to Ramsgate or Margate to see the sea and enjoy an afternoon at the seaside.

'I didn't have a pessimistic outlook and in the end I got a marvellous job in the camp because I and another friend were in charge of the bicycle shed. That was a real bonus because it was shift work, every third day you had completely free as long as you attended your English lesson. That means you were almost out of the normal discipline and it was really enjoyable. You could read a book and improve your knowledge of English so it was a good stroke of luck when this job became available and I and a good friend of mine were sharing it.'

As the situation in Europe worsened, more and more refugees arrived at Richborough and in the nine months prior to the outbreak of war in September 1939, the population of the camp rose to 3,500. The Camp Director placed great emphasis on the teaching of English at the camp as well as giving guidance on English customs and etiquette. This coupled with the fact that the majority of the refugees were educated and skilled men, meant that the newcomers were popular with the townspeople as Alex Howard of Canterbury remembers:

'After a while we were allowed to go into Sandwich, which is a beautiful little town. I had a smattering of English from schooldays, and the people in Sandwich were charming, in fact I was more or less adopted by one family, Mrs Saunders in particular was wonderful. She became my future mother-in-law, I was invited to their home and they had a young daughter who later on became my wife.'

Not even the little town of Sandwich was free from the grip of fascism, and Philip Franks recalls that members of the British Union of Fascists were present there.

'There were some black shirts in Sandwich and Deal and around who used to come past the camp with their flag to maybe intimidate or upset us and they even had meetings in Sandwich so our Camp Director didn't allow us on that day to go into Sandwich, because we knew there would have been a brawl, we couldn't stand that. There was a very small toll bridge between the camp and Sandwich so it was easy for us not to go in.'

When war broke out, travel through Europe became almost impossible and the refugees stopped coming to Richborough. The majority of the men were eager to enlist in the armed services to help defeat Hitler, many of them joining a unit which gloried in the name of 'The King's Own Loyal Enemy Aliens' which was put to work on Kent's coastal defences. At first the War Office was reluctant to involve the refugee recruits in more important duties, but after it had interviewed all the men to check there were no likely Nazi sympathisers in their ranks, the Auxiliary Military Pioneering Corps was formed and trained at the camp. Alex Howard was among those who joined the Pioneer Corps:

'Not on the first day of war, but within a fortnight, British Officers arrived — Majors, Colonels, Sergeant-Majors and Sergeants — who started to drill us. We were given rifles without ammunition because although we were friendly aliens, we were aliens. We had drill every day for a number of hours so that was my very first experience of army life.'

The inhabitants of the Richborough Camp were all men aged between eighteen and forty, but many Jewish children came to Britain, thanks to a scheme called the 'Kinder Transport'. The Home Office gave permission for the Quakers and other organisations to rescue the children. At the end of July 1939 Fred Dunston, after almost three months in the Richborough Camp, was given Home Office permission to become an administrator at a transit camp being organised for these children at Great Egham Farm in Ashford. Fred was a Group Scout Master in Austria and prior to coming to England had been busy organising Jewish children who were forbidden to go to school. Fred felt very privileged to be able to help the young refugees who were trained in agriculture before being moved to other parts of the country or abroad.

John Ullman from River was only a child when he was rescued from Stuttgart by a Quaker lady. As in many such cases, luck played a large part in John's escape from Germany and it was his enthusiasm for stamp collecting that almost certainly saved his life.

'My mother was walking down the main shopping area and I saw this English car in 1938, very low slung with GB plates on. I ran over and my mother told me off for running away but I went to the lady who pulled the window down and I said to her in English, "Do you have any English stamps?" She took an envelope from her handbag, I expected her to tear the stamps off the envelope but she gave me the whole envelope with her English address.

'If I hadn't had that I am convinced that my sister and I wouldn't have been here to tell the story. I think I might have perished with the other six million. It was actually the Quakers who got many of us to safety and I was one of the fortunate ones who were helped by the Quakers.'

Like many other Jewish refugees in England, John joined the Army as soon as he was old enough to enlist. After coming through the ranks of the East Kent Regiment, the Buffs, he was put on special intelligence work at prisoner of war camps, at Stanhope, near Ashford, and Langdon Barracks in Dover. John, although a man of Kent by adoption, chose to serve in his home county.

Blanche Donovan, Air Raid Warden, in her
fire-fighting uniform.   (B. Donovan)

Members of the Borough of Gillingham Fire Brigade at Gillingham Park for the Dedication
of their fire engine 'Plewis' on Sunday 9th April 1940. On the far right of those mounted
on the first level is Claud Evernden.   (Kent Fire Brigade Museum)

Chapter II
DUTY CALLS

At the end of August 1940 the call up of reservists and volunteers gained momentum and many Kentish people had rejoined the Civil Defence Movement for a variety of reasons, as Gwen Devereux explains:

'I was in the ARP in 1938 when they first started. We'd always been interested in first aid, my brother-in-law was in the local Margate ambulance corps. My sister and I took up the Red Cross later on and trained for two years before the war started. It was the ARP which had the responsibility for checking the blackout which people were practising occasionally during the summer of 1939.'

Blanche Donovan volunteered as an Air Raid Precaution Warden: 'I moved to Gravesend and didn't know anybody so I thought I would use my time and join the civil defence. In 1938 we were given an area of Gravesend which we would be responsible for; we had to know everybody in each house and also whether there were any invalids, so that if and when war came we could be sure they were well looked after. I was the only lady in the first class but eventually we had one or two more lady wardens.'

Ken Geering was another early volunteer joining the auxiliary fire service: 'Around about 1937 things were very unsettled and it was quite obvious to most of us that there was going to be a war. I was attracted by fire fighting, I thought it was the best thing to join. Fire fighting was a very popular part time job in Ashford, we had the oldest volunteer fire brigade in the country and many of my friends were members of the main volunteer brigade, that is what attracted me to it. It was to a degree dangerous, though not as dangerous as some people think, and it was exciting. It was also a good social mix of people.'

Air raid wardens became a familiar sight in their navy blue uniforms and white tin hats at the beginning of the war and the duty that most people remembered them for was enforcing the blackout. Some people thought that the wardens were over zealous in this task as Walter Bevan recalls:

'It even got to the stage when you were told off for lighting a cigarette with a match. Whether they could see from five miles or three miles up I don't know, but you were told in no uncertain terms that you'd got a light showing and not politely I don't mind telling you.

'I remember one chap who always had a light shining through a kink and the Home Guard threatened to put a bullet through his front window. They got very strict, actually I think they were over the top, they had been given a bit of position and they reacted a bit too strongly.'

Enforcing the blackout was considered a vital job and the air raid wardens took their duties very seriously as Blanche Donovan recalls:

'There was one person living quite near to The Waterloo and night after night I had to go and say: "Your curtains are not right". One night somebody rushed in and said, "There's lights across the road again," so I said "I've had enough, I'm going to summons," but I couldn't summons without a policeman to back up the stories. We had a PC Winter; if ever anyone was in trouble he came along. He came along that evening and I showed him the light. Well when I had to go to court I felt so sorry, it was the lady herself that came, her husband was a very bad-tempered Irishman, he wouldn't go. I did feel sorry, she was fined £2. On the Sunday morning I was off duty and helping out behind the bar in The Waterloo and I saw this same man strutting across the road. I said to myself, "Aye aye, I'm going to get a black eye". He came and ordered his beer and I put my hand out for the money and he grabbed my hand and shook it and said: "Congratulations on doing your duty." Another night I was walking along Wellington Street and in one house was a naked light, if ever there was a signal this was it.

'I'd got a warden with me and we went to the front door and banged it; no answer, so we went round the corner to a side entrance and opened the gate. There was PC Winters and he said: "You in trouble again?" and we both climbed in the window. Thank goodness it was off the latch. I was thrilled with myself, I'd always wanted to break into a house, I wish I hadn't. I've never seen a room with such filthy bed linen, no beds, it was all on the floor. I don't know how many could have been sleeping there. The stuff was filthy and it reeked so we quickly took the globe out to put out the light and we got out of the house straight away. So I'd achieved something I'd wanted to but it wasn't very pleasant.

'Another night on a Saturday night, someone complained that the barracks had a light on. That was nothing to do with the wardens, that was down to the service but to console them I said I'd just go over and mention it. I did put my steel helmet on before going to let them know I was official. It was a pitch dark night but I knew my way; all of a sudden a voice yelled, "Halt, who goes there?". So I replied "friend". He put his torch on and I was inches from a bayonet.'

The emergency committees of each local council had the job of arranging both the recruitment of ARP staff and also their accommodation. It was often a problem finding sufficient premises for the warden's posts. In Gravesend the post was moved from the Wellington Arms public house up to The Waterloo, which was considered far better accommodation.

Blanche Donovan points out another hazard for wardens:

'Eventually we had another sandbag post beside The Wellington Arms which I objected to because rats from the railway used to come in. Finally we had a brick one built.'

During the phoney war ARP recruitment and training continued but there was criticism from some quarters about the amount of money the government was spending on its civil defence programme. In October 1939 the city of Canterbury was the subject of critical investigation by the Daily Mail, the headline read: 'ARP — is your town run like this?'.

'Daily Mail investigates the bomb budget of Canterbury. Canterbury Cathedral city of twenty-five thousand people, considered by the defence experts to be one of the safer cities in the country, has just received its first ARP wages bill which comes to nearly six hundred pounds per week, which means thirty thousand pounds a year if war goes on. Thirty thousand in wages per year for the protection of a city of twenty-five thousand people, believed to be so safe that when war broke out they rushed more than one thousand five hundred evacuees here from the crowded areas.'

The negative attitude towards civil defence soon changed when the air raids began in 1940 and the ARP commanded great respect in the community on the efficient way in which they handled emergency situations.

For those who wanted to join the regular services, conscription was introduced within minutes of war being declared and the National Service (Armed Forces Act) was enforced.

This meant that all fit men between the ages of eighteen and forty-one were now liable for military service for the duration of the hostilities. 93% of those who had attended the compulsory medical examination were considered fit for active service. Conscientious objectors, nicknamed 'Conchies' by many soldiers, were forced to attend special tribunals which had the task of deciding whether it was justifiable to excuse them from military service on pacifist or religious grounds. For many the problem was which service to join. Some, like Ronald Allen of Gravesend, had the decision made for them:

'While I was at school my big ambition was to get a short service commission in the RAF but my father, who was flying in the 14-18 war, talked me out of this saying that would only last for five years and what would I do after that. I wanted to become a pilot with Imperial Airways but still he talked me out of that one. As it happened, at one of the cinemas the local Territorial Army Search Light Unit had a display in the foyer and as I came out I thought if I'm not going to join the RAF, I'd join an anti-aircraft unit and that was the reason I joined the TA.'

Ron Cattell from Aylesford decided to join the RAF at sixteen straight from school rather than the Army because of his father's experience in World War I.

Horsmonden Auxiliary Fire Service at their H.Q., with their converted Morris 6. Ernie Wood is to the far right in the front row. This photo has been autographed by Wing Commander Bob Stanford-Tuck, a Biggin Hill pilot whose Spitfire crash was attended by Ernie Wood.

(E. Wood)

'My father served in Salonica and just before the second war broke out he was taken seriously ill and lost the use of his legs for eighteen months through deprivation, because the soldiers were literally eating shoe leather in Salonica.'

Jack Browning was also very young when he volunteered to join the Navy. When war was declared he was working at a garage in Ramsgate and says:

'I can remember my mother coming across the forecourt of The Star Garage and she was crying. "Oh Jack I've got your calling up papers," she said. I was full of the joys of spring. I was called up on my sixteenth birthday and into the Navy I went. I joined at Chatham, I was a Chatham rating.'

The day the call up papers arrived was the start of a new adventure for many but after the initial excitement, the strict rules and regulations of service life came as a shock to the new recruits, not least of all because many of them were so young and had never lived away from home before.

Ron Cattell recalls being kitted out. Articles of daily clothing were issued free of charge and included items with such wonderful descriptions as, shirts angola drab, drawers cellular and drawers woollen.

'These things you see on the films from those old days weren't far from the truth as I remember it. We simply joined the queue and were then sized up, according to what sizes of clothing we took, for example what size shoe or hat and if you did not know, the quartermaster simply said, "That's a nine" or "That's a fourteen" or whatever and you carried the whole lot, a collosal pile, it was literally thrown at you. So many shirts, so many vests, so much underwear, top jacket, uniform best blue, boots, cap, hat, all the lot, and then you took that back to the barracks. It was a race then to see who was quickly into uniform and therefore, officially the first. If any of the guesses of the sizes of clothes were wrong we had to go and change them but with the uniforms themselves, there was a tailor available who made the alterations, very rough and crude ones I must say. The other traumatic experience was queuing up for the barbers, as one of the first things you had to do was have your hair cut short. I had fairly long wavy hair, there it was just literally a matter of taking the razor right the way across the back of the head and down, and there was your hair, gone. From then on you had to keep it regulation short.'

The new recruits soon discovered that rules governed every aspect of daily life. Ron Cattell remembers:

'One thing that sticks in my mind is gun fire at the crack of dawn where if you wanted to you could get up and dash down to the side of the barrack square where they had a table laid out with urns of tea, you just filled up your mug and went back. You had to have your own mug, your own knife and fork, your own irons as we called them, and we very quickly got into the habit of sending one chap, who was very keen on doing it, down with a bucket and getting a bucket full of tea and coming back and serving it all around the barracks. Immediately after Reveille, we had to be out onto the square for early morning PT in shorts.'

Colin Cuthbert from Margate considered himself quite independent when he joined up:

'I went to St John's Wood Air Crew Receiving Centre and I'd always been, even when I was young, my own boss and it was quite different having someone say, "My name is Corporal Garthside and by golly you're going to remember my name," and I thought "My God, he's right". I've never forgotten it.'

A few weeks spent in training camp, despite the restrictions, have always remained some of the happiest times for those who fought during the Second World War. For Ron Cattell it was the excellent training he received as an RAF Apprentice that has always stuck in his mind.

'What they did was to give a thorough engineering training in all the various specialist skills. Nowadays everybody does everything, but then it was

Harry Eede in the centre of the front row just after his promotion to Battery Sergeant Major. (H. Eede)

separated into aero engines, radio and air frames. Our first experience of flying, we had to have experience of flying because we had to do air testing, and my particular group were moved to Cranwell for six months. We did our first flying in an old Vickers Valencia which is a First World War bomber with an open cockpit, cabin behind, a bi-plane with two engines. I remember one of the engines stopped before we were taking off, the flight sergeant jumped off the wing and literally cranked it up again and off we went, did our stint around and came back down and as soon as we landed the engine stopped again, so you could look back on that and laugh.'

Not everyone was lucky enough to enjoy the benefits of full training, however. Ronald Allen, who was a member of the 313th Kent Anti-Aircraft Company, found himself on active service before the war had even been officially declared.

'The calling up papers arrived during the evening of the 24th August 1939, that entailed a trip to the drill hall at Pelham Road at Gravesend and then we went by bus to Beaux Aires Detling and arrived at 1.30 in the morning and took over the site from the unit that was there at dawn. Almost immediately we went into what was known as an emergency night run and then, as far as I was concerned, there was guard duty for eleven hours straight off with only an hour's break.'

Claud Evernden became an instructor to the AFS and was based at Gillingham during the war. In addition to his duties as a fireman he was also responsible for maintaining the air raid sirens in the area.

'I was a service electrician for the Gillingham Corporation Electricity Department, based at the old power station in Windsor Road. I always had an interest in the fire brigade but when I joined it was difficult to get in, there was quite a long waiting list. For young people in those days, it was the prime thing in the town. We were training these AFS men and some of them turned out to be very good firemen indeed. There were ladder drills, hose running drills and learning how to use all the equipment that was provided which was coming along in those days very, very slowly.'

Kent's young people joined the volunteer movement as well as adults, as Margaret Collins remembers:

'As a very keen Girl Guide I was able to go and do quite a lot of voluntary work, one of the most interesting duties was at the town hall. At that time, Maidstone was an area to receive evacuees and in preparation for this, various information offices were set up and people came into the town hall for information. We directed them to various places and to welfare organisations. Just before the war broke out we scrubbed quite a lot of the houses along the London Road, there were many large old houses which are hotels today and they had stood empty because of the depression. They were taken over by the council and we scrubbed them out to get them ready for pregnant mothers and mothers with small children who were to be evacuated to the town.'

Ruth Wilson was only sixteen when she became involved in war work:

'I started in the council offices in Faversham, I was on holiday and my father as acting town clerk recalled me home. My first job was to go around all the appropriate shops and check on the number of blankets they had as they would be required for the evacuees.'

Young men were not to be outdone by the young women as Walter Bevan remembers:

'We were all in the Scouts in Longfield, the local scout group, and we volunteered our services as messengers. What we had to do, nobody had any idea, but we volunteered.'

Stanley Day of Gravesend was an apprentice in 1938 and war seemed imminent to him then because the reservists were being called up:

'I didn't want to stay an apprentice all my life, so I went to the Admiralty in Whitehall in March 1939 and signed on. Three months later I was told, "You can't do that you are a bound apprentice," so I said, "You can argue with the Admiralty". In the end they let me go and I was sent to Chatham in July. We were given half a crown (12½p) and I thought I was rich with half a crown a day, I was only on five shillings (25p) a week then as an apprentice. We had to pay one shilling (5p) for our dinner and in Chatham then you got buns and milk for tea break until the war started then all that changed.

'We started to learn to swim. We had to swim three lengths of the baths and tread water for three minutes in a white duck suit, whether you could swim or not didn't matter, you had to jump in the deep end and if you went under that was just hard luck. I finally got through that. We did square bashing, boxing, boat pulling, physical training. Of course in those days discipline was very strict; if you didn't obey the leading hands anything could happen. One morning we didn't get up on time, we were all late, so the following morning we got a roll call at five o'clock, told to lash our hammocks up and there we were doubling around the parade ground with a hammock above our heads for two hours. We were never late after that.'

Although limited conscription was introduced in the spring of 1939 principally to establish anti-aircraft defences, there had been a steadily rising number of volunteers for both the full time and reserve forces as Martin Mason, a 17-year-old from Dartford, remembers:

'During the week before war, many people I worked with who were old enough to be in the Territorial Army had gone on their annual camp, for many of them the only way they could get a holiday at all was to join the Territorials. Ever so many of them went and didn't come back until after the war, several of them didn't come back at all and quite a number of them were taken prisoner at Dunkirk. I went for a medical to try and get into the Navy but was told I was needed where I was at the moment at work and to go back, which I did. A friend of mine went at the same time and he did get called up into the Navy but I never did.'

Dick Rose was another who tried to enlist even though as a sub-ganger on the railway at Lyminge he was in a reserved occupation. 'I was on the Elham Valley line, second in charge of sixteen men which was quite a big job at my junior age. I wasn't called up because I worked for the railway, but I tried to join the regular service and I got sent back and told off.'

Freddie Cooper found the call up process rather muddled:

'The electricity company for whom I worked in 1939 encouraged us to join the reserve services and many of us joined the RAF because there was a recruiting office in Rochester High Street, right opposite. We used to go to Eastchurch to do our training. I was called up a week before the war broke out, demobilised three days later and I thought the war was over. I was called up again the day before war broke out and given six stations to choose from with the RAF. I went to Manston which was my first choice, I got there and on the night before war was declared we were told we were moving off next morning to South Wales.'

Blanche Donovan had rather a more successful start to her career in the ARP. She describes the training:

'We had to go into the hut with our gas masks on and have them all tested and then see how well we could run in our gas clothes on the prom. In the case of a raid there was always one person at the end of a telephone and every night even before the war, we used to do a bit of patrolling to see what was happening.

'That kept us busy because working all day I only had Saturday afternoons and Sunday mornings, so there was quite a few months work. When we practised first aid, we had to pretend that we really had had a raid. I had the pleasure of giving the boss of my firm the kiss of life.

'When the gas masks arrived I had to take them round and fit them on everybody and look for faults and there were faults, pin holes mostly, and then replace the gas masks. The children loved them, they thought it was fun trying them on but the adults realised what they really meant. I must say I prayed we would never have gas. The baby masks were huge things, difficult for any mother to cope with. I personally put a baby in a mask because the mother couldn't do it.'

The fire service was a vital part of civil defence in Kent during the Second World War, as fires caused by German incendiary bombs caused more structural damage than normal high explosive bombs. In the months before war broke out the government and local authorities held a vigorous recruiting campaign for people to join the auxiliary fire service. It consisted of volunteer firemen from all walks of life, many of whom were unable to join the regular armed services. They were trained by existing fire officers supplied with the minimum of utilitarian equipment and put on stand by to assist the regular fire service.

Ernie Wood's unit in Horsmonden, for example, had a homemade fire engine, as he remembers:

'A local fireman had produced an old Morris 6 saloon car which our crew converted. He cut the top right off and made it into a miniature fire engine with a manual pump on the back, plus a cabinet place for the men to sit on. In the storage place we carried all the hose and we carried forty gallons of

Lena Marshall aboard one of the RAF's 'Cole's Cranes'.
(L. Marshall)

water, that was our complete unit. Our uniform consisted of boiler suits, three axes between us, a tin hat and wellington boots and that was how we were equipped. The fire engine was kept in the old garage at the Kings Arm Pub and our sleeping quarters were in the old stables there.'

Albert Kidgell from Cranbrook joined the auxiliary fire service and remembers his introduction:

'I'd just been married and we'd got a flat near my mother's place so I thought if I join the fire service to train I'll have a night off now and then to go out with the boys. When we trained we had to climb ladders, firemen's lifts, knocking down targets and learning all about fire pumps and pressures, what to do, how to enter a smoking building. Really and truly once we got into the blitz, none of that counted.'

Ken Geering's training in Ashford was equally intensive:

'All the time we were training, training, training. At that time we were allowed to go out to civil fires which were anything from fires in a haystack to fires in a house. We were rather second class firemen, we were supposed to watch what the full time men did. We were being trained on aircraft recognition, on bombs, what sort they were going to use, we were trained on ordinary and incendiaries and then a particularly horrid type which happily I never encountered, with an explosive nose. They also had butterfly bombs which had delayed action, which were rather like a can of beans with the flaps which opened and they fluttered down and would get lodged in gutters. I can't say I ever saw one of those, but I heard talk about them.'

Wartime fire stations operated along similar lines to those of today in which the telephone was central to the emergency procedure. Mary Hilliker from Sittingbourne was among the staff at Dartford Fire Station.

'We had to learn to become telephonists first, then to be able to use the mobilising board and despatch engines to different areas, to Canterbury, Rochester or Folkestone. We were always on the alert and we were never allowed to use shorthand, we all had to write in clear handwriting. This was most important so the firemen could read and see what we were doing.

'Immediately a call came in, down went the bell and we directed the firemen out.'

Many of the men working with Mary were part-timers and there were sometimes unusual volunteers:

'One little one I remember clearly, he came to sign on as a part time fireman and I looked at him, he had no arms. I thought, how am I going to cope with him but he just put his foot up, signed his name. He was a clever man, the jobs he did for us were amazing, off would come his shoe and out would come his foot, he really worked very hard.'

Claud Evernden was a part time fire worker during the war and he remembers the call out procedures:

'Those of us from the pre-war Gillingham fire brigade had house bells and they were worked in conjunction with the maroon that was fired, this was like a giant firework. If we were out at work we heard the maroon and if we were at home we heard the bells and went to the station on standby. From there we were sent to various incidents that happened anywhere in the borough.'

The neighbourhood fire watching scheme epitomised the community spirit that was so common among people during the Second World War. Where the ARP was unable to set up a scheme, people often set up their own. Walter Bevan was one of the fire watchers who were organised in Longfield:

Members of the Searchlight Crew at Beaux Aires, Detling, known later in 1939 as 'Sleepy Valley'. Ron Allen is seated in front of the Officer.   (R. Allen)

'There was a meeting called at the school by the headmaster asking for volunteers to become fire watchers. I was fourteen, I thought I'd be too young but I went with my father and neighbours. We were split up into sections of three and given orders as to which part of the village we had to patrol and what night we would patrol and that was it. We had nothing, I had my First World War battle bowler, a tin hat that I had scrounged, which I stuck firmly to and went patrolling three nights a week with my father and a neighbour.'

When Harry Eede was called up in 1940, he quickly found himself in the front line working with the coastal gunners based in Folkestone. His job was to try and prevent the German army penetrating inland should they manage to reach the Kent coast. He worked 24 hours on the guns, 24 hours in reserve and 24 hours off, heeding the advice received from his father:

'He was in the First World War and he refused promotion but he said to me if you get a chance of a stripe or anything, go for it, because if you make progress in the Army, you'll find the money gets better and also your life gets easier. So I put myself out and I had very quick promotion. I was a sergeant within eleven months and a battery sergeant major in eighteen months.'

Conscription was not introduced for women until 1941 but it was anticipated by Lena Marshall from Canterbury who could not wait for her twenty-first birthday when she could join up without parental permission:

'The German army had swept straight into so many areas and covered so much ground I said to win this war they'll soon be calling up the females as well as the men. Everyone laughed and said they will want volunteers of course, but don't be ridiculous, they won't be calling up women. I was so certain they would. My friend and I spoke about it and decided we would have to do something and we would rather do something before we were compelled to. We said it would have to be the RAF because we could see Manston from where we lived and we were aware of the RAF.'

Discipline for the women was no different from that of the men as Lena remembers:

'You had to fold all your equipment and it had to be all neatly displayed, your shoes had to shine, the blankets had to be put in their proper order and wrapped around with another blanket and the sergeant major would come around and inspect them. Your buttons had to be polished with Brasso and you were supplied with a button stick made of brass and you put your buttons on it and polished them like that.

'One of the things that sticks so clearly in my mind is that we attended a lecture about hygiene and I remember a woman saying, "At the end of the day, if you cannot wash lisle stockings then turn them inside out and hang them out of your windows so the fresh air gets through them for the next day."'

After completing her training she was posted to Detling and served there in the winter of 1940:

'They were short of drivers and one of the things I had to do was drive an old Dennis type of cattle truck with a canvas over it and a brass starting handle to wind it in the front. I spent, it seemed, years driving the butchers every day to Chatham Barracks to collect rations. It was so cold at night that when we got back to dispersal point, the radiator had to be drained. In the morning it was such a panic as there was only one tap in the yard for all of us to use and you had to remember to wind up the Dennis beforehand to get the oil going round the sump.'

After serving in Detling which was one of the Kent airfields heavily involved in the Battle of Britain, it is the camaraderie of the time that ex servicemen and women remember today as Lena Marshall sums up:

'The very fact that we were all undergoing the same experience and it was an absolutely new experience, it forged a bond, we were all equal.'

These road blocks on Maidstone bridge clarify the fear of Arthur Nash, living and working on opposite sides of the Medway, that he might be stranded on 3rd September 1939.
(Kent History Centre)

Chapter III
THE DAY WAR BROKE OUT

Everyone alive the day war broke out can remember where they were and what they were doing on that day, Sunday 3rd September 1939. It had been a long hot summer and after storms the previous night, the morning of the third dawned calm and sunny over the whole county of Kent.

Walter Bevan aged fourteen was sitting in his garden in Longfield when the announcement came:

'Us lads just sat their quiet, nobody said a word, all busy with our own thoughts. All our fathers had served in the First World War and my thoughts flew straight to my father. Having been an avid reader of First World War stories, I could never contemplate how they stood the horrors and the terrible conditions they had to fight in and I thought they did their share, now it's our turn to do our bit and how would we compare with them. Suddenly one of the lads spoke and said what thousands of lads probably said in 1914. How long would it last? Would we get into it? And if so, which service would we go into? My special chum and I grinned at each other, we knew it would be the Royal Navy for us.

'While we were talking the alert went and the sirens sounded. We jumped off our feet expecting to see hoards of German planes flying overhead and one of the lads said, "Crickey, that was quick".'

Joyce Bishop, a sixth former at Dartford County School, recalls:

'When war broke out I was visiting my grandmother and we expected it, we knew Mr Chamberlain was going to broadcast. I was sitting with her and it came over the wireless. I can recall looking at her and she began to cry. Of course tears weren't available for me, I'm afraid, I just consoled her and went up to see my great grandmother, who was alive, and told her the news because she didn't have a wireless. From there I walked home. Walking home on that Sunday morning, the air raid sirens went and then fear did strike me, I thought "I'm here walking along the road and there's an air raid, what shall I do?" I remember I ran home and that is very vividly inscribed in my mind, the fear I had then.'

Mrs Evelyn Wilson from Birchington was also visiting her grandmother when the news was broadcast:

'My grandmother's reaction was a result of her experience of the First World War. She said "We will all have to have hot Bovril now as we won't get one for years." She remembered the shortages.'

Fred Hadlow from Canterbury:

'I can remember sitting in the living room, listening to the wireless with my feet in a bowl of water. We heard the message from Neville Chamberlain and almost immediately afterwards the siren sounded. We looked at each other thinking "What do we do now?". Nobody really knew and my young brother said, "Put a blanket up to the window, that will stop the flying glass," which we did. And then the warden for the district came popping round on his cycle shouting, "Air raid Mrs Hadlow, air raid."'

Chrissie Gallivan was working as a telephonist at the ARP Headquarters in Chatham Town Hall when the announcement came. She remembers:

'I was on a six to two shift in the cellars beneath the town hall. Captain Cain was our Chief and I was manning a telephone connected to the warden's post and we all listened to the wireless for the declaration of war. There were about twenty of us there and we all had telephones connected to the warden's posts. A few minutes later my phone rang and we all thought it was the first air raid of the war, but no it was the warden's post from Christ Church and they were asking why they hadn't received any tin hats, so we all relaxed after that.'

Ken Geering from Ashford was also on duty at the time, he was with the Auxiliary Fire Service:

'It happened that I was in the ARP Headquarters building at the time. We also had a fire station there and I remember when we heard Chamberlain say we were in a state of war with Germany, we all went outside expecting the bombers to come over the horizon.'

Mick Johns of Hadlow, a five-year-old, was sitting with friends and family in their garden in Pembury when the alert sounded:

'We thought immediately that the Germans had started invading and therefore we had better get out of the garden. We all rushed indoors and a few of us burst into tears, including me, thinking it was actually a German bomber because we could hear the aircraft, but we couldn't see it.'

Eileen Dykes from Dover remembers her experiences:

'I had gone to Sunday School, my father was out, he was an electrician and he had the job of going round with his workmates to take the lights out of the street lamps for the simple reason that the Government knew that there would be a war.

'I remember coming home from Sunday School and sitting down and listening to Neville Chamberlain's speech. Afterwards mother said, "Oh well nothing's going to happen now, we're alright for a while. You can go down and post a letter". Lo and behold the siren went. "That's only to say war has broken out," said my mother. So I went toddling off with the little boy next door in a pram and got to the caves and this policeman came out and said, "Come on over here, there's a war on." I said, "Well yes I know there is." He replied, "There's a raid on as well, get in the shelter." I said, "But I haven't got my gas mask." I was in an awful panic, I was only twelve years old and I had this little boy with me and he started to cry. There was an old lady in there and she said, "Haven't you got your gas mask?" The all clear did go pretty sharp, I never did post mother's letter. I went straight home in a bit of a panic. All my mother said was, "You'll always have to take your gas mask with you."'

The first siren of the war turned out to be a false alarm, given because an unidentified aircraft was seen approaching England. It was a friendly civil plane flying in from France, but to everyone who heard the warning it was real enough.

Stanley Day from Gravesend was a naval reservist stationed at Chatham Dockyard at the time:

'The siren sounded and we were in swimming. The instructor said, "Right, take your trunks off and put a towel round you, put your boots on and run across the parade ground to the tunnels on the other side." So off we went, dashing across the parade ground, the WRENS had just formed up and one chap dropped his towel, and the WREN following behind had a laugh and there were blushes in all directions. We got to the tunnels and the instructor told us all to get dressed and so we did and then there were giggles from below us and all the WRENS were standing watching. In the middle of it somebody shouted gas, which caused rather a panic because half of us didn't have our gas masks.'

Bobbie Stacey of Folkestone had four young soldiers billeted with her family a few days before the war broke out.

'My mother said, "Don't get another job, please, until they've gone because I shall need you to help". So four very hungry, very healthy boys were with us and I spent half my time peeling potatoes.

'I even remember us all hanging around listening to Chamberlain's speech and as soon as he had finished, my mother dashed over and opened the window saying, "We must be able to hear if the air raid alarm goes" and of course it did. It was the false alarm that everybody made an awful fuss about."

Margaret Collins of Maidstone was a fifteen-year-old Girl Guide, helping with preparations for war in the Town Hall:

'We listened in the Mayor's Parlour to the declaration of war and immediately afterwards all the sirens went and the Mayor got very agitated and sent us down into the cellars to take cover. He dashed out onto the Town Hall steps and directed people furiously, "Get under cover," he shouted. Everyone was gazing round looking to see if there was a plane coming over.'

Ruth Wilson was the daughter of the Faversham Town Clerk:

'I was feeling very unwell on that day and my parents went to the ARP Head-quarters. All of a sudden the siren began to blow and our siren got stuck and instead of the usual sound, it kept on and on, frightening people.

'My parents sent a car for me to join them at the ARP but when I got there I suddenly realised I had left the gas on in the oven as I was cooking the dinner, so someone had to go back and turn the gas off.'

Chamberlain's announcement came in the middle of morning church services. Martin Mason from Dartford and Joyce Rayner from Faversham were among those who were in church at the time. Martin Mason:

'I was in one of the local Methodist churches in Dartford and the service had just begun when the air raid siren sounded and everybody rushed out of church. When I got outside people were rushing in all directions and we heard that Mr Chamberlain had announced that war had begun.'

Joyce Rayner remembers:

'The day war broke out I was in the parish church, and they obviously gave the announcement. My father came rushing into the church to collect me because the siren started going and nobody knew what was going to happen. I was taken home where we had prepared one room with streng-thened windows and sealer round the door in case of gas and we just sat in there until we heard the all clear go. That was how the war started for me.'

George Cawte, a young evacuee in Tunbridge Wells, remembers:

'We'd been evacuated a few days before war broke out and in that short time we'd managed to make contact with other families and other children living in the area. A family quite near to where I was billeted were church-goers and they organised a little group of us to go to church. The bonus was we were taken by car. There were no cars in my family at all so, of course, the car ride was worth it; even if I hadn't perhaps wanted to go to church, the car ride was great because it was a novelty. We went to church on the road between Southborough and Tunbridge Wells. Just after the service started, the siren sounded and the Minister announced from the pulpit that war had been declared and so we were all sent home. We were rather worried about what was going to happen.'

Many clergymen had made arrangements to be told the news that broke during their services. Mabel Jenner of East Peckham had the job of bearing the message to her local church.

'I was at home with my mother and we were doing our ordinary Sunday jobs when the announcement came about war breaking out. I went down to the church and saw the verger, my uncle, Mr Hope, and I gave him the message. He told the vicar, the Rev. Bassett, straight away. The vicar stopped the service and gave special prayers. Everything was quiet for a few minutes, I think they were expecting it, they just bowed their heads and joined in with the prayers.'

Barbara Letchford was in Canterbury Cathedral attending a service when the siren went so she went down to the crypt. She remembers a lady in there having hysterics because she couldn't get her gas mask on and was shocked. 'As a child I had never seen a grown up having hysterics.'

Gladys Townshend remembers being in chapel in Goudhurst:

'The Prime Minister had been over to Germany and Hitler had promised there would be no war and of course it was quite a surprise. I lived about a mile from the chapel and on Sunday mornings about eight or nine little children used to go off to Sunday School at ten o'clock in the morning. Around ten to eleven, I used to get my cycle out and collect my mother from her home and she and I walked to the chapel. Suddenly about five to eleven there were lots of whistles blowing and shouting, of course there were Londoners here for hop picking and they used to love to accumulate in the village pub for a drink in the morning.

'A man came into chapel and they took him up to the preacher and the preacher said, "I'm sorry to say that war has been declared against Germany. Any of you here who haven't brought your gas masks or feel you would like to go home do so!" Quite a number left and I gathered these children and we went.

'Outside it was bedlam, there were people rushing down the road, the Londoners were saying, "Oh these bleeders". Awful words actually, worse than that. "They are probably bombing our homes in London at this very minute."'

'I dashed home with my mother as fast as I could get her to move. I took the children home through a field and it was quite comical really, we'd had a gale a day or two before and a tree had blown over and I had to get all these children over the fallen tree to get to the path. When we were almost at the main road, we saw the girls from the college here running back to the air raid shelter, they had white panama hats on and you could see all these hats on different sized children bobbing along, everybody was rushing. When I finally got the children home, because they all lived handy, my next door neighbour had already boarded his windows up in that short while. He was a bit panicky. He took it down afterwards because nothing happened.'

On that Sunday morning, Michael Fitzgerald, a Londoner, down for the hop picking season, had already settled his own wife and family into their hut at Five Oak Green and was preparing to bring down more of his relations from London to join them. He recalls that morning:

Walter Bevan knew on the day war broke out that he wanted to join the Royal Navy. He achieved that ambition in 1944 at the age of 18. (W. Bevan)

Michael Fitzgerald, who drove to London and back to Kent on the morning war was declared — in spite of the air raid warning. (M. Fitzgerald)

'I went back to London to pick my brother and his wife up and while I was there the first sirens went. There was panic stations everywhere, everyone was flying about, I just got in my car and went to my brother's place, picked him and his wife up and made it off to the hopping. As we were going along the road, the police stopped us and said, "Go and take shelter." I said I was in the ARP on the way to the depot, anyway we got through the Blackwall Tunnel, out onto the Kent Road and bang, we carried on straight down here.

'When we got to Five Oak Green most of the women were in the pubs talking about the bombs that were coming so they were all crying. "Oh you got back safely and all that, what's it like up London?" "Same as it is here," I replied, "nothing's happened yet. That was only a siren."'

Don Crisp, a recent young evacuee to Deal, was enjoying a change of lifestyle:

'On the morning of the day war was declared, a gorgeous morning I remember, my sister and I were paddling in the water not having had too much experience of paddling before, when the siren went off. Panic-stricken, not only us but everyone else in Deal, we raced off the beach down to our temporary home in West Street, plimsolls in hand. I was bearing no thought for my younger sister, she was looking after herself. We

44

eventually got to our billet and the poor old dear we were billeted with was stretched out in the hallway surrounded by neighbours, having had a heart attack, so we weren't ever so welcome on that occasion. We moved the following day.'

Arthur Marsh, a Maidstone man, was working as a baker at the Co-op in John Street. He worked on continuous night work from eight o'clock in the evening to four o'clock the next morning and from four o'clock in the evening to four o'clock in the morning each Friday. On 1st September 1939 the bakers were informed that all the roundsmen who delivered the bread had been called up and so the bakery asked the production workers for volunteers to go on the delivery rounds. He takes up the story:

'None of us had driven an electrical vehicle before and the roundsmen's books were not very helpful. Some had customers names and no numbers and others had numbers and no names. We struggled on not knowing the route, we ran the battery units right down, so you can imagine how we felt by six o'clock in the evening of the Saturday, having been thirty hours on our feet, we were dead beat. At that time I lived in Upper Fant Road. When I got up I read the Sunday newspaper and the headline was "There will be no war".

'Well we all heard Mr Chamberlain and know what he said so I wondered what I ought to do when the all clear went. I went into the little garden we had at the back of the house and dug like fury and had a lovely trench. I went off to work that night with enough food to last because I thought I might not get back over the River Medway. When I finished work in the morning at four o'clock, I met a policeman who told me of all of the rumours of what had been happening in the night. I walked down my garden path and promptly fell straight into the trench, I'd forgotten all about digging it.'

As far as Bert Lewis from Sittingbourne was concerned, Chamberlain might never had said a word. He remembers:

'The day war broke out I was going to Dover with a pal of mine. When we arrived at the station there was nobody there, not a porter, no one. We walked out into the street and there wasn't a soul about there. I said to my pal, "Seems dead." "Yes," he replied, "Isn't it quiet." All of a sudden a policeman turned up and he said, "What are you doing here?" I said, "We are on holiday, we've come for a day's holiday." He said, "Don't you know there's a war on?" I replied, "There wasn't when I left home." He said, "Where's your gas mask?" I said, "That's in the front room at home." He stated, "Well you're supposed to be wearing it, what are you going to do now?" I said, "I didn't know," and he said, "Come on down the station."'

'So down to the police station we went and he kept us there until two o'clock. He then told us we could go. We were getting a bit hungry and I said to may pal, "Let's go and see if we can find a café." We couldn't find a café, then we did find one with the door open and in we went. A lady came out wringing her hands saying she had no food and nothing cooked and then shut the door telling us we would have to go. I said to my pal again, "Let's go down the front and see what's going on down there."'

'There were very few people about and we got up to the harbour and the Navy was there. I thought I'd take a few photographs as I had my camera. We found somewhere where we had a good view and took these photos. Luckily there wasn't a policeman around then or I would have gone straight back to the nick again. We couldn't get anything to eat anywhere so we thought we had better go back home. We were very hungry by the time we got to Sittingbourne.'

Doris Ayres, a teacher at Maidstone Grammar School for Girls, was also on a train when the news came. She was on her way home from Leningrad after a holiday in Russia. She recounts her tale:

'I was alone, the only English woman on the train. There were a lot of soldiers and various other people who were very kind to me and attentive, fetching me all sorts of things every time we stopped at a station. Going to fetch tea. At one station there was a great commotion on the platform and a soldier in my carriage rushed out and bought a newspaper and showed it to several people and they all got terribly excited. I wondered what was the matter but I couldn't understand. The soldier disappeared down the long coach and came back accompanied by a lady who spoke French and told me that England had declared war because Germany had invaded Poland.

'She told me a little bit more, but not much and then I was really horrified because when I left England I didn't dream that anything like that would happen. I knew that international affairs were rather dodgy but I had the chance of touring in Russia and I took it.

'The train went on and we arrived in Moscow where there was a great commotion, all sorts of people, English, Norwegians, all gathered together, all trying to find some way home. I joined a group of English men and women, about thirty all together, and we saw various officials who couldn't do much for us. Tourist guides were very good and installed us in a hotel. We waited a day or two and then they offered us a passage as far as Sweden in a cargo boat.

'The people of the English party were well looked after by the Russians on board the boat and we arrived in Stockholm, after which the Swedish authorities sent us on to Oslo in Norway by train. By this time my money had run out but the British Consul was unable to help us. After a day in Oslo the party was sent on to Geilo which was half way across to Bergen, a big ski resort right up in the hills, but the hotels were shut, it wasn't the skiing season in September.

'They opened two hotels for us, a small one and a large one. I was in the party put in the large one and we stayed there for about a fortnight, going out every day tramping up in the hills and amusing ourselves the best we could, fraternising with the villagers who again were very kind. We did some stupid things, we women got so bored that we unknitted some of our jumpers and knitted them up again for something to do with our fingers. The men played football and they wore their boots out so the village cobbler mended them for nothing. It was really a glorious holiday, if only we hadn't been so bothered about people at home and how we ourselves were going to get home.

'We invented a war newspaper in which we put silly stories, cheering up news and cartoons and we kept it up for a fortnight. We really did get very anxious and then we discovered the people in the small hotel had somehow wangled their way to a ship so we were furious and wrote to our Members of Parliament. By a miracle the letters arrived in England; mine went through to the Maidstone MP, Alfred Bossom. We demanded a war ship to take us home as we were important teachers, doctors, railwaymen and miners, all sorts of people including students in this party and we thought it was important that England should get us back so we waited . . . no answer, then at last we all received exactly the same letter on House of Commons notepaper saying they were doing their best to get us home.

'We waited a little longer and then we were told they had found a way of getting us home. They took us overnight on a train to Bergen on the west coast of Norway and we stayed the night in a sailors' hostel. The dining hall where we had our supper in the evening was plastered with notices show- ing maps of the mine fields in the North Sea which didn't comfort us very much. We had already heard that London was flat! Anyhow we were loaded onto a lovely looking small ship, a sort of yacht affair, somebody said it belonged to the Kaiser and he used it in the First World War in the Kiel Canal. It was alright but it wasn't very sea worthy.

'We crossed the North Sea and it was pretty rough and everybody amongst the passengers except myself were sea-sick and some of the crew were ill too. There was a doctor on board who came from Scotland and I was very friendly with him and his wife and I toured around the ship holding a tray of lemon drinks behind the doctor feeding the crew as well as the passengers. We had a scare because an aeroplane kept passing on the horizon, we thought it might be a German, it was too far away to see. Then we picked up a boat load of fishermen who had been threatened by a submarine and they had a man with a badly injured hand, so everything on board was very exciting.'

The day war broke out had turned into an adventure for Doris Ayres lasting several weeks. When the boat eventually docked at Newcastle the passengers were thoroughly vetted by the British Authorities before being allowed to travel to Kings Cross overnight. From there Doris ended her long journey by travelling to Maidstone to take up her duties at school as an English teacher.

After the excitement of the siren sounding that morning, the first day of war continued without incident. There was anxiety about the future but the work of digging shelters, preparing the garden for autumn, planting and sowing and improving the blackout blinds still had to be done.

Peggy Jenkins, evacuated to Smarden from Croydon, spent the day preparing for school.

> 'I don't quite remember how we found out the war had broken out, but we heard the church bells ringing and we knew this would be a sign that the war had started. Everybody went quiet and I went out into the farm yard and looked out over the five bar gate and thought, "What does this hold for me? What is war about?" I didn't exactly seem frightened but it seemed a little bit lonely.'

There were mixed reactions to the news that Britain was at war. Those who remembered the terrible suffering and losses of the First World War were filled with dread at the thought of another similar conflict. Others treated the news with a mixture of apprehension and excitement of not knowing what the future held.

At six o'clock on the evening of 3rd September, the wireless once again became the focus of attention. King George VI spoke to the nation giving a message to all to stand calm and firm and united in this time of trial. He continued, "There may be dark days ahead and war no longer can be confined to the battle field. We need to be ready for whatever service or sacrifice it may demand and then with God's help we shall prevail.'

The weather deteriorated as evening closed in and many of those who had missed church that morning made an effort to attend the evening service. The BBC later bulletins brought the news that France and Australia had entered the war but there was little fresh information, except that petrol rationing would begin in two weeks.

Before retiring to bed people in Kent, as all over the country, checked that their gas masks were packed ready for work or school the next morning. With the blackout in force the county lay in darkness as the day war broke out ended peacefully.

Chapter IV
THE EVACUEES REMEMBER

Preparations for the evacuation of the civilian population were under consideration as early as 1938 and Kent County Council not only had to organise evacuation within the county, particularly away from the Medway towns, but also prepare to receive some one hundred and forty six thousand Londoners from the south and east of the city. Accordingly, Reception Officers, Billeting Officers and Co-ordinating Traffic Officers planned the exercise with surveys and schedules covering transportation and accommodation.

By the end of August 1939 war appeared inevitable and the evacuation operation was implemented on 1st September 1939, the day Germany invaded Poland. Although the number of evacuees arriving in the county were fewer than expected, the annual influx of Londoners to Kent's hop fields took place on the first Saturday in September, a tradition over a century old, which only served to add to the inevitable confusion. The story Jim Stokes retells illustrates just some of the problems:

'We were assembled at The Mathematical School (then in the High Street) at Rochester, preparing to march to the railway station to be evacuated to Canterbury. The thinking then was that Canterbury was a safe area of evacuation as it was an open city with a cathedral and the head of the Church of England there. We got on the train at Rochester and off at Canterbury with no trouble. We were then allocated to our various houses. They took three of us fourteen-year-olds to the other end of Wincheap, up Cockering Road, and presented us at the doorway of a very nice lady and gentleman, who were unfortunately expecting about eighteen month or two year old babies to look after. They got quite a shock when we turned up at the time, because we looked a bit hungry, but as was the case in the war, people never refused a cry for help and we were taken in, one of us for only one night, then he was re-allocated. My friend and I stayed there for quite a while and made ourselves at home.'

Nine-year-old Barbara Letchford was also evacuated from her home in Chatham to Canterbury:

'One of my big problems on 1st September was that we had got all our gear to take on the train to Canterbury. I had a packet of egg sandwiches which my mother had packed for me and that first evening I sat at the dining room table with these sandwiches and Mrs Hall asked me if I was worried about

Leonard Smith evacuated from Gravesend to East Dereham, Norfolk, is pulling the barrow, helped by his brother, Roy, collecting salvage. (L. Smith)

something. I said I didn't know how long the sandwiches were to last so I didn't know how many to eat this evening.

'She smiled and explained that from now on she would actually be feeding me and that was part of the undertaking but that to me was a major problem. My problem wasn't that there might or might not be a major war, my problem was egg sandwiches.'

The Southern Railway ran twenty-seven special trains on two days from the Medway towns with the larger group going to the Sittingbourne and Milton areas, about five thousand children in all. Some Kent school children were lucky enough to go by sea as Leonard Smith who was then aged thirteen-and-a-half and in charge of his two younger brothers and two young sisters remembers:

'We all congregated at the Gordon School, Gravesend, on the Sunday morning about half past eight. We were advised as to where we should go and what we had to do. We marched from the school with all the mums and children crying and carrying on, we went aboard the *Golden Eagle* at West Street Pier in Gravesend and just before the *Golden Eagle* sailed the town band played Auld Lang Syne. All the boys thought we were going on a great adventure, we thought we were going to win the war. At about eleven o'clock when we were off Sheerness, we heard the announcement by

Neville Chamberlain that war was declared and then we had a destroyer escort to Yarmouth. We stayed the night in a school having straw to sleep on. They gave us a bag of food which we were supposed to take to our future landladies but all the kids went for it, chocolate, cakes, everything that was edible they had it.

'During the night an air raid siren went, everybody panicked because they thought we were going to be blown to pieces, so they took us all down in the shelters. The following morning we were taken to the villages and towns. I went to East Dereham and when we got there we went to another school and were lined up like blooming slaves. They came around and selected the people they wanted.

'My brothers and sisters and me had decided we weren't going to be separated on any account, but nobody wanted to board five children, we were standing there right to the last. Then we decided we would have to split up. My two sisters and myself went to one house and my two brothers to another. In the end they were very kind people and they did what they could for us. It was total freedom, we were out in the country and we had a lovely life for the first few months — out walking, for us coming from Gravesend it was so free, we had no little jobs to do, it was childhood as it really should be. Occasionally we used to get a letter and we might get a postal order for a shilling (five pence), to split between us.

'As time went on you did start to feel homesick. Some of the children whose parents could afford it would come and visit them, but my father was away at sea and my mother couldn't afford to come here so we didn't see anybody really. At that time Norfolk was really in the country and you never went short of anything.'

Ted Jenkins from Northfleet was almost thirteen years old and a pupil at Gravesend County School for Boys at Milton. His school held evacuation rehearsals during August and his departure date was also 3rd September. At 4.30 am he and his father cycled to school in the dark. He takes up the story:

'My father carried my kit bag containing a change of clothing, washing and writing materials and food enough for forty-eight hours. We embarked on the merchant vessel, *Royal Daffodil*, at West Street Pier together with pupils from the Girls County School, the Junior Tech, the Convent School and other local parties. The Mayor, the Town Clerk and the headmaster were there to see us off.

'We picked up a naval escort and learned that our destination was Lowestoft, Suffolk. Once on the open sea the ship's motion got the better of many and this was not helped by the issue of free cold milk.

'In Lowestoft one thousand children and staff were lodged temporarily in the Odeon Cinema until the following Tuesday. Volunteers fed us meat sandwiches, milk and fruit. We learned there that war had been declared and the first air raid alarm had sounded while we were still at sea.

Eighteen months later, aged 14, Leonard Smith went to sea as a Cabin Boy. It shows how quickly children were forced to mature in wartime.   (L. Smith)

'In the evening we had a film show for our entertainment and then we settled down as best we could for the night, some slept in seats or on gangways, some on the stage or others perhaps most comfortable of all on straw in the entrance foyer sharing what rugs were available. That night adults, mostly women, went round comforting the younger ones, particularly during the false air raid alarm at about 3.00 am.

'Sanitary arrangements were difficult. There were about four wash basins and as many toilets for nearly a thousand children and adults in that cinema. On the Tuesday morning we went by bus to Beccles, for us the last eight miles of our evacuation journey had taken more than forty-eight hours.

'I was in a group of twelve boys who initially went to a large house, a hot meal of stew awaited us and was very welcome after three days of cold meals. Only then was a check made to ascertain that we were all from Roman Catholic families as requested by our hosts. As this was not so, several of us were taken to other villages, including my friend Reg and me. We had a large bedroom each and a recreation room, fully furnished and provided with indoor games and a record player, mostly classical records. We also had our meals there, they were brought up two flights of stairs by the maid, a young person who cycled several miles across the Waveney Valley every day to work.

'We were very well cared for and treated like guests in the house but not an integral part of the family. We had no indication whether our hostess had children of her own. She had, however, a high regard for good manners and behaviour and patiently corrected our faults. We were allowed to go out in the evenings but had to return by 9.30 pm.

'Not long after we arrived, letters passed regularly and I received a letter or a small parcel every week with pocket money, sweets, clothes and the local newspaper. Such was the number of postal orders in circulation that shops locally were allowed to accept them as currency.

'In late September school lessons began again at the church school room, YMCA hut and various other places. We spent our weekends walking for there was much to see on the river and marshes and on Sunday mornings many boys attended the special ten o'clock service for evacuees. We had regular meetings with our housemasters to ensure that we were all well and comfortable in our billets, writing and receiving letters and an opportunity to discuss any other problems. In addition a sick bay was set up and run by the masters' wives and everywhere we went there was the gas mask to carry, at least in the early days.

'On the very few occasions when the siren sounded at night we would go down to the cellar. This was very neat, clean and equipped with a stirrup pump, sand and a small stock of emergency food and fresh water. Our hostess would come up to our rooms and talk in the evening, I remember her showing us the correct way to shake hands with ladies, this being different from that with a gentleman, how table cutlery should be laid out and things like that. She also believed that vinegar on salad was not good for us and insisted we had lemon juice instead. Only one incident marred our stay with her, my room on the top floor was lit by gas and after I was in bed the light would be turned off.

'In case of an air raid it would be turned off at the main gas tap. However, one evening my lamp was forgotten and it began to leak gas. It was still dark when I awoke with a thumping headache. After I opened the large sash windows the gas soon cleared. My hosts were quite shaken when they realised what might have happened and how serious it could have been, so alternative arrangements were made at bed time.

'As Christmas approached the question of the holiday arose and since there had been very little war activity, it was agreed that we could go home for two weeks. At this time a number of boys returned home permanently. Our hostess decided that since we would not be sharing their Christmas dinner with them, she would give us pre-Christmas lunch during the last week of term. This was a full dinner, partly of our own choice, poultry, sauces with all the appropriate table arrangements including a gift of very good quality leather gloves for each of us.

'We were late back to school that afternoon and on our return there was a Christmas tea laid out for us, including nuts and fruit for the evening. Such kindness is not forgotten. We went home nearly one hundred miles to Gravesend to be met with tears and tell all our tales. Our second departure back to Suffolk in January was almost as sad as the first.

'During the autumn of 1939 the staff and local authorities had made great efforts to find suitable accommodation to house our entire school of three hundred boys under one roof and finally a disued Poor Law Institution was chosen. This was a workhouse such as Dickens would have known, later on

Dorrie Smith's class from Gordon School, Gravesend, singing hymns before boarding the *Golden Eagle*. (L. Smith)

we found the old Day Books in the attic, daily records of the poor and the travellers, the work they did and what food and shelter they were given. It was all redecorated, kitchens put into working order and it was planned to open the new school on 1st January 1940. It was obvious then that we needed cycles and mine was sent up by goods train. For those without transport, the Norfolk County Council helped by providing Norman Cycles at low cost or to rent and issued waterproof capes and leggings for everyone. Then came the snow and every boy wrote home for rubber boots and gloves. Riding those three miles to school became impossible so we walked, lessons beginning at 10.00 am and ending at 3.00 pm to allow us to get home by dark. The snow remained until mid-March, often with high drifts and blizzard conditions; many boys managed to make sledges to ease the journey.

'Shortly after Christmas we had to move to another billet as our previous hostess was unwell. We moved to a medium sized house with three bedrooms on a council estate and were given a very warm welcome. It was obvious that this was to be a very different home from our previous one, here we were to be an integral part of family life.

'As I remember it took a week for our shyness to disperse, in fact our hostess thought that we were unwell, however we quickly settled down and as we grew up so did our appetites.

'At Easter my friend Reg returned to Gravesend and another boy called Ernie was billeted with me. We both helped Mr Linger on farm work through the summer, ditch clearing and hedge cutting, after which he would sell the cut wood as pea and bean sticks and share out the profit. Those bill hooks were like razors.

'In the summer of 1940 my mother spent a much-needed two weeks holiday with us, staying in a house on the same estate. My father's job at the paper mill was a reserved occupation and he was exempted from military service, but my mother was not only welcome here, she was almost feted like someone from the battle zone which indeed she was. When the time came for her to return she was presented with gifts and produce of all kinds, too much to carry. By this time we boys had acquired the local accent, a fast Suffolk/Norfolk lilt which initially my mother had difficulty in understanding.'

Meanwhile in Kent, preparations were being made to receive children from London who were evacuated on the 3rd, 4th and 5th of September in 1939. Winifred Baker lived in Platt near Sevenoaks at the time and recalls:

'Well I just remember that we made preparations to receive them in the Memorial Hall and we had mothers and children and school children, boys and girls. I had a thirteeen-year-old whom I think came from Plumstead; I don't know whether she was a child from a broken home, she didn't seem to have a father but she had a mother and the mother used to come down occasionally and stay with us for the weekend. She did quite well but she had very London ways of eating, everything was out of a tin. She knew what a cabbage was and I do remember one thing stuck in my mind, that we'd had the opportunity to get some very good victoria plums and we'd all hoarded sugar before the war. I made quite a lot of plum jam and this child said she hated plum jam, she couldn't eat it, so I renamed it damson and then she thoroughly enjoyed it. That's why they were difficult to feed, because they weren't used to our way of eating things out of the garden and things that were fresh. We had a big vegetable garden at that time so it was quite easy to make a little go a long way.'

Margaret Collins from Maidstone also remembers her Londoners; Alfred, Eric and Ernie Bell from Plumstead:

'We had three little boys, and they arrived with hardly any clothing to their name, very unused to our way of life, baths and so on and they caused quite a lot of entertainment in our family. They enjoyed going out into the country, which was of course quite new to them, and soon found that scrumping was a very happy occupation. They didn't stay with us terribly long and moved on to Mangravet I think at that period.'

Ruth Wilson recalls the administrative problems:

Pupils from Catford Central School for Girls were evacuated to Smarden with their younger brothers and sisters. This photo was taken in the playground of Smarden Village School when the Mayor and Mayoress of Catford, together with an LCC Education Officer, visited Smarden in March 1940. (K. Morris)

'We were inundated with evacuees and for some unknown reason there was a muddle and some of the poorer type of child went to the better class homes where they didn't originally want to take evacuees so they were sent back quickly. In some cases the child wet the bed or wouldn't eat. Anyway, in the end we got it all sorted out and I think they were quite happy.'

Lilian Parkes was living in Ivy Hatch near Seal. Her husband was a gardener and handyman of a large house which belonged to a Sevenoaks dentist who left just before war was declared and had no choice about whether or not evacuee children came to live in his house. Lilian had sixteen evacuees from London placed with her without any warning, as she remembers:

'There was a knock on the door of this big house and I opened the door and there was the billeting officer pushing all these children into the hall. So I had to make some beds and all that for them and get them into bed. I think there were sixteen or maybe thirteen and three of mine. They started from four up to fourteen which wasn't really right. One family there wouldn't sleep on a bed, they'd never slept on a bed before so they refused to get into it. I had to lift the mattress off the bed and put it on the floor and they were alright.

'It was a big country house and there was a horse and paddocks, a couple of dogs, greenhouses and fruit trees and they went completely mad stealing the apples. We had two bathrooms. My husband used to bath the boys in one and I used to bath the girls in the other. I don't think they were used to having baths every so often. We had a very good person down at the bottom of the drive of this house and she used to send up a pail of milk every day. The cowman would come up with it for the children, my goodness me, that was a help.

'I had a large enamel jug of cocoa for them for breakfast and sometimes when they came home if they were hungry. They had bread and butter pudding done in the oven with milk and sugar and I had no help in the house except my twelve-year-old daughter who got fed up with all the washing up. I worked jolly hard I might tell you, I was up at six o'clock in the morning and got to bed at twelve midnight. Half of those children only had the clothes they stood up in and I used to wash, dry, iron and air them so they had the clothes for the morning. I earned that pound a week I might tell you.

'Buying a leg of lamb for Sunday lunch cost four and six pence (22½p). My husband took the boys for a walk on a Sunday morning to get them out of my hair while I cooked the Sunday lunch. He took them to a big farm to see the cows which he thought would be interesting for them. One little boy came back and said, "I didn't like that farm, we have our milk in bottles not from a dirty old cow."

'One of the children was moved to another billet later and he came up to see me after he had been billeted and said, "I've got a smashing place." I said, "Have you Jack, what's it like?" This is what Jack replied: "I have bread and jam for breakfast, bread and jam for dinner and bread and jam for tea . . . it's smashing."

'And there was me cooking them great big milk puddings, rice puddings, big jugs of milky cocoa, I'd worked hard, washed and cleaned, but then I did get a letter from the Queen and my husband had a letter from the Queen. I was the only one in the village to have such a letter thanking me for what I had done.'

Although few people can have experienced Lilian's baptism of fire, one child could be equally as demanding, as Gladys Townshend from Goudhurst remembers:

'They came round and asked if we would have evacuees and I'd got room for one, as I already had two sons. They brought him round on a Saturday, it was a very hot day and he came, this little chap. I shall never forget him, he had curly hair and an old cardboard box with his gas mask, little trousers below his knees which were supposed to be shorts and some plimsolls with a hole and his toe peeping out.

'Fortunately I'd got clothing from my own sons and the younger one's just fitted Ronnie and with a pair of shoes I hadn't collected from the local repairman he was quite a gent. He was pleased to be in a home again and he got on our settee and jumped over the arm and said, "I'm clever aren't I?" I said, "Yes, but don't do that any more Ronnie, that's to sit on."

'He said, "It's just like my mum's at home but we've got a brick under ours to keep it straight." Poor little chap. The following Sunday his parents came to visit him and they were proper dockland people. The mother had a white pinny on and the father had a kerchief around his neck, they were very pleasant. They had a cup of tea with us and after they had gone, the kiddies were talking and my boy said to Ronnie, "Your dad doesn't wear a tie, does he?" "Yes he does," said Ronnie, "he had his tie round his neck. He doesn't wear one of your ties, but he wears one of those other sort."

'The following week the parents came again and they were quite dressed up, but when the Battle of Britain came, one Sunday his father and mother were visiting and they said they never had anything like that in London and they took him home straight away.'

Evacuation at this stage was completely voluntary but not all children returned to their parents because of the dangers as Margaret Collins explains:

'At the beginning of the war the billeting fees were paid entirely by the Government but when things were better organised, parents were required to pay a contribution and it was then that a number of early evacuees were taken home.

'I don't think they were too badly off, probably better off than my parents were. The first time they visited, we gave them afternoon tea and generally made a fuss, but when my father pointed out that the boys' shoes needed repairing and they replied, "Oh well, can't you do it for them?" we began to have other ideas about our generosity. When the parents next arrived they were asked to wait outside and the boys were delivered to them.'

Complaints were made to the authorities as Ken Geering, who was working for Ashford Urban District Council, recalls when Ashford residents were moved to Oxfordshire after Dunkirk.

'There were quite a large number of letters of complaint and as a result, the council sent the Deputy Town Clerk and me up there for about a week during which time we visited almost all the people who had sent in complaints. It was difficult for them in the sense that if you are billeted with somebody you can't get along with, your life can be pretty miserable. In the main they really were homesick, both the mothers and the children. We didn't find anything very serious, we did find some marvellous, wonderful people doing a fabulous job, especially the WVS who were looking after them. They took great care in whom they put with whom and they visited the houses. One woman in Banbury had organised a club for them in a very short time so they could get together and that was fairly typical.'

Kent was the reception and billeting area for thousands of children, although at the outbreak of war only about a third of the expected 146,000 arrived. The coastal towns in Kent were classed as suitable for the reception of evacuees as Don Crisp experienced:

58

'The Gordon School in Eltham where I was educated was evacuated down to Deal in Kent, which seems rather a strange place in retrospect, bearing in mind that war was just over the Channel. We went down by train from Charing Cross, the whole school, and when we came out of the station in Deal we lined up, a long snake of snotty-nosed kids I suppose, with gas masks and cardboard cases, clutching the remains of sandwiches and oranges. We walked down the road from the station to the seafront and we went to the Gordon Hotel, just opposite the pier, in the ballroom surrounded by the local gentry and housewives, rather like an auction with all the kids in the middle, completely bemused.

'We were selected by various people until there were only a couple of fairly unacceptable kids left, those two kids being my sister and me. But we were eventually chosen to go along with some poor old dear in West Street, I seem to remember, where we were billeted. That was two days before the war started.'

George Cawte also came from South London into Kent.

'In the week before the war, I was evacuated along with quite a few other boys from Fossdene Road School in Charlton and went down to Tunbridge Wells, in fact Southborough.

'Although I don't remember much about the journey down, I do remember arriving at the village hall in Southborough where we were given sandwiches and refreshments and sorted out into little groups ready to be taken around to various houses. As a thirteen-year-old, the house I went to seemed a bit on the posh side, especially to me who was living in a council flat at home and hadn't many of the luxuries that this house seemed to have. We were made welcome. I'll tell you how I think it was posh, one day we were sitting at breakfast and we were asked if we would mind wiping the basin when we had finished. I thought that meant the lavatory pan, and I certainly didn't fancy wiping that around every morning, but of course gradually I began to find out a basin was a wash basin. We called it a sink at home.

'After a few weeks I was transferred into High Brooms and billeted with a school caretaker and his wife and three children. It was a different set up altogether, more of a family and I settled in very well. One of the things we had to do after school was go up and help clean the classrooms, sweep up, empty the waste paper baskets and that sort of thing. It was a great life and I can honestly say I enjoyed that part of the evacuation.

'The war really didn't mean anything to me, there was nothing much happening and the jobs we had to do weren't very great but I found them good.

'The one thing that did used to worry me was that during the war, if there was an invasion, the signal was to ring church bells and school bells and I had a horrible vision that one night I might be turfed out of my bed and made to run up the road with Germans coming down from the sky with

Ted Jenkins seen here with his 'foster parents', Mr and Mrs J. Linder, in Bungay.
(E. Jenkins)

Ted Jenkins evacuated to Bungay, Suffolk, is pictured with his mother who had a welcome holiday from Gravesend.
(E. Jenkins)

parachutes to go and ring the school bell, because during the winter of that first school year, the caretaker was unwell and his eldest son had started work. I was the next eldest and so it was up to me to go up to the school and unlock it in the mornings, so you can imagine every night I used to lay in bed and think, "Please don't let any Gemans come tonight . . . I don't want to go and ring the bell."'

If George Cawte thought his first billet was posh, imagine being a child who ended up living with a real life princess. Doreen Bradley from Sutton at Hone was only six years old, evacuated from South London.

'I was one of four children but nobody could take four and the vicar said to everyone, "You've got to do your best, you should take them in." So the other people waiting said to him that he would have to do his bit too so in the end he was pressurised; he didn't want to but he did take my two sisters. So they split us up, the two eldest and the two youngest.

'Somebody came and took us to a great big house, it was a mansion and was lovely. When we got there we were introduced to a prince and princess. He was Russian and she was English. I first remember she said, "You're tired because you've had a long journey," and then she had a wonderful plate with a dish, all posh to us because there were six of us children, and on it she had cream and redcurrants, all fruit, then we had to go to bed whether we wanted to or not.

'We were treated very well, much better than my other two sisters where they had to go to church three times on a Sunday and in the week. When we were younger you went to church when you wanted to, our mum didn't say we'd got to go. There was a mission hall and if we wanted to go we could go. We used to go to visit them, the Princess took us there and sometimes they came to us. We had to write home to our mum and let her know we were alright, it was an experience I shall never forget.'

Peggy Jenkins who was then aged eleven had the long journey from her home in Croydon to the middle of rural Kent, the village of Smarden. She was accompanied by her elder sister, Kitty, who was fourteen, a friend Valerie and her young brother Jimmy who was twelve. She describes their experiences:

'My poor brother had to be evacuated with us because my sister was the eldest and she could look after him. He was taken from school, away from all his friends and had to join all these girls. On the morning we left, we packed our cases, it always seemed such a long way to walk to the edge of the estate and mother trailed with us, taking the three of us down to the bus station. We stood there with our cases, gas masks and little parcels and my mother sat us right inside the bus on the three seater and by the time we got inside with our cases, she sat down and cried. The conductor said, "What are you crying for love?" She replied because we were being evacuated and he told her not to send us. She said she must as it was for our own good.

'In the school playground we said goodbye to our friends and I suppose it was the best way out that my mother didn't come to the station with us. We caught the train at Hither Green station and, on the journey, if that train stopped once it must have stopped a hundred times; we kept asking the teacher, "Where are we going?" and she said, "I don't know." There were no signs on the stations because they had been blacked out. By the time we arrived we thought we had done three hundred miles and there we were in the middle of Kent at Charing, probably forty miles from home.

'We were taken by coach to the village hall and then divided into three groups. We went to Smarden. Every child was issued with a carrier bag which contained a tin of milk, a tin of corned beef, some biscuits and a great big brand new blanket. We were taken on to Smarden Village School where we all assembled and were given tea and biscuits. We met a woman there called Mrs Sharpe who seemed to do all the organising of evacuees.

There were several people with her saying, "I'll have two or three or four,"; we seemed to be getting left until the end as there were three of us and my sister's friend. Presently this large Mrs Sharpe, who was always an angel, said, "Leave those four children to one side, I will take them." We were the last to leave the hall. We were placed in a taxi and taken up to Park Farm, where we met Mrs Wood, little Mrs Wood who was as small as Mrs Sharpe was big. She stood there all four feet eight or ten of her with these huge wellington boots, which I swear were her husband's, and her clothes right down to the ground.

'She smiled and said, "I'm pleased to see you," then she trailed us in with our cases. We went through the scullery and then through where they had their main food, where there was a big inglenook fire place and through another door to a small sitting room.

'We trailed up the little wooden stairs, through Mrs Wood's bedroom, through another bedroom which was to be my brothers and into the bedroom which was to be ours. In that room was a great big four poster bed. It may sound as though it was a wonderful place, well it was to us, but the furnishings were absolutely tatty, everything was falling to bits, the carpets were falling to pieces, so I commented, "What a lot of holes in the carpets," and all the other three children said, "Shhh."

'Anyway, we unpacked our clothes and went downstairs and had, as always, bread and butter, cheese, jam, bananas, cake, whatever we liked. I felt quite safe and secure in that place. It wasn't luxurious, but I knew we would be alright and happy here. Mrs Wood lit all the paraffin lamps and the candles and we could hardly see. She then thought it was time we went to bed. My sister and I climbed into the four poster bed and our friend Valerie was put in the room beyond, but it wasn't long before she came in with us and from then on all three girls shared the four poster bed.

'In the morning Mrs Wood brought some water up for us to wash in and we heard it splashing in Jimmy's room then she came into us, still with her wellington boots on. Two buckets full of water with water boatmen floating on top and the water was absolutely black. Still we washed and cleaned our teeth in it.

'This was Saturday September 2nd, but we had no idea whether war had broken out, there were no papers or wireless, nothing, but Mrs Wood said war hadn't broken out because the postman had been and he would tell us anything. We spent that Saturday exploring the hay barns and the farm which my brother and I thought fantastic. I think my poor sister had the job of sorting out our clothes and doing any washing, but my brother and I really enjoyed ourselves.'

Evelyn Wilson, who lived in Chatham, went to Ham near Eastry for about a month after war was declared until France fell, when they were all to be sent to

Wales, but her mother thought that would be too far to travel so they went back to Chatham. She recalls:

'I lived in a farm house at Ham with no running water, no electricity, a pump in the yard, oil lamps and a loo down at the bottom of the garden with a bucket . . . very different from home. We had great fun playing on the farm but it was a long walk to the school in Eastry and 1940 was a hard winter; just the same, I was sad to leave there.'

Evelyn Cundy taught at Catford School for Girls and was also evacuated with her pupils to Smarden. She remembers how the children looked when the time for evacuation came:

'Some of them were looking very apprehensive and their mothers were looking very apprehensive too, all the labels round their necks, they had to carry enough food for a couple of days because nobody knew where they were going to end up. Those were the confidential instructions we had been given. It wasn't far from my school at Catford, we caught the train to Charing, the train journey was completely uneventful. From there we went to Smarden and one contingent went to Bethersden. In the school were a whole number of village people waiting, very apprehensive also I think, to know what they might be going to catch. They didn't know whether they would be getting toddlers or grown ups or children from a desirable area or children from a less desirable area.

'Looking back it was absolutely marvellous of them to undertake a "blind date", which they did. "I've got room for three", "I can take one", "I'll take a couple of sisters". When the children were sorted out, they started on the staff. I remember I did kick at being asked to share a bed with another member of the staff and said I had never shared a bed with a stranger. We started off in a lovely Elizabethan cottage and were told the site was first occupied during the Wars of the Roses and had been rebuilt under Elizabeth. We stayed there for a couple of months.

'The majority of children remained as evacuees and those that did and were homesick were very brave children. They bore it and didn't let it show too much. One does what one can, but one really doesn't know what happens in the evening or at night when they are by themselves. You can notice if a child is off colour during lesson times or if you meet them later, but you don't really know, you can only guess. I wanted to do my very best for them, we all did in our various ways, whatever we could do. That meant giving up a great deal of our spare time, I suppose that's what teachers are for.

'We always seemed to get the troubles when it was just dark and preferably when it was raining. You would get a knock at the door, Mrs whatever her name was, says she can't have me any more. Then we would have to go frantically through the list of people who might, at a moment's notice, take children in, or maybe you had to go and say, "Couldn't this be smoothed

Don Crisp's mother had this photo of him taken just before he was evacuated to Deal — fearing that she would never see him or his sister again. (D. Crisp)

over?" It was generally a bit of tantrum or something and the answer was usually, "Yes, we will have another try."

'I couldn't praise too highly the people who put up with an influx of strangers for those five years. I cannot because of what it must have meant to them, I can't gauge but I can guess.'

Not all children were evacuated for the entire five years of the war, and nor were some evacuated within the school schemes as Margaret McIntyre recalls:

'I was evacuated three times during the war, when we lived in Beckenham. The first time was the very night war broke out and I was only about four and a half but I remember so clearly because I had gone to bed and in the middle of the night my father woke me up. He, in discussion with one or two neighbours, was quite convinced we were going to be invaded by the Germans immediately. We were literally picked up in the middle of the night, wrapped in blankets in the back of the car. We had a car because my father was a commercial traveller, not many people had cars in those days. Together with another neighbour, who was also a commercial traveller, we were going down to Wiltshire to stay on a farm which belonged to a relative of this neighbour. My father and the other fellow were quite tired because they had both done a day's work. Suddenly we were woken up with a thump in the back, the other driver had fallen asleep. Fortunately the damage wasn't terribly serious as we weren't going too fast. Eventually we arrived in Wiltshire.

'We stayed there about six weeks living above a grocer's shop. It was a little holiday for us and of course nothing happened so we came home again.'

Some parents could not bear to be parted from their children, including Beryl Cooper from South London:

'I finally decided after yes, no, yes, no, for a few hours that I was going to send them. They were all ready and when I let them go I had a few tears, naturally, but all of a sudden I thought no, I won't let them go. I cannot be separated from them. I rushed down the stairs and met my husband and I sent him to go and get them. He just took them straight out of the line and brought them back with their big tickets on. It was a fairly important organisation around here, evacuation, every school round about, about ten whole schools had gone. I brought the children back thinking I'd rather not have them separated from me by being evacuated, but if trouble came I'd have them with me, so I decided the only possible way of getting them out of London was to take them hop picking with me. So off we went.'

Gwen Devereux of Margate also suffered mixed feelings: 'We hated our children going away, especially my younger boy. He was a real "mummy's boy". I gave him three postcards, stamped and addressed, so that he could write to me now and again. All three of them came about a week later by the same post. The first said,

"Dear Mummy, I'm crying because I want to come home."

The second:

"Dear Mummy, I miss your cuddles, I want to come home."

While the third read:

"Dear Mother, Don't write, send a telegram and get me quick!"

He thought he could come home by telegram!'

Dolly Taylor from Strood was a child whose parents would not allow her to be evacuated and she remembers:

'I was eleven the day after war broke out, so I was due to go up to Gordon Road Senior School. There were no arrangements made for the children who stayed at home. Most children had been evacuated. The school decided to send a teacher round to our homes and she came with school books, set up homework and she came back the next week to mark it and correct any mistakes we had made and leave us more work. This didn't go on for very long, I think they must have found it impractical because she couldn't get round all the houses in one go. They decided we'd go to the school nearest our home which was Temple School for Boys in Cedar Road, which was the first time I'd been to a mixed school. Classes weren't very large as many of the children were away.'

Joyce Bishop from Dartford was a sixth former at Dartford County School at the start of the war and recalls being involved in pre-war preparations and the disruption of education.

'I had to go to Westgate Road School to help pack 1,208 carriers of food and our return to school was delayed for some time; we kept getting little notes saying we would return on such and such day, and then eventually it was cancelled.'

Margaret Collins, a fifteen-year-old pupil at the Maidstone Grammar School for Girls, remembers:

'At the beginning of the war we hardly went to school at all, which was rather devastating because this was the start of School Certificate Year. I think we went two afternoons a week and received lots of homework until the air raid shelters had been dug and blast walls put up. Then when we did go back, we had to welcome Kings Warren School from Plumstead who were evacuated to our building and billeted round the town.'

Doris Ayres, a teacher at Maidstone Grammar School for Girls also remembers:

'When I got back to school they had no shelters and as the school was shared with Kings Warren the children were going to school on alternate days and having work set to do at home. We didn't dare have the school absolutely full with no shelters at all. Later on Kings Warren School left because it was considered too risky for them to stay, but lessons continued at the Grammar School on alternate days until they did manage to dig some trenches.'

Joyce Rayner from Faversham recalls that evacuees had an adverse effect on her own education:

'It was very disruptive because we weren't allowed to have the whole number of children in the building at one time, so we had some of our lessons at the institute in Solomon's Lane. We weren't at school all the time, we had staggered hours because everyone had to have some schooling.'

Rosemary Huckerby from Maidstone remembers another disadvantage:

'Sometimes in the classes there was a mixture of different ages, particularly when children were evacuated away.'

Catherine Taylor from Stockbury Valley was at school in Sittingbourne when war was declared and she also remembers the evacuees:

"In my case and the case for a lot of other children, we were in part-time school, in the first year of the war, of all things we had evacuees down from the suburbs of London and nobody knew what was going to happen. They were here for about a year and of course they had to have schooling so they shared our school. There were no shelters at that time.'

George Cawte, evacuated to the Tunbridge Wells area, describes his schooling:

'School was very disruptive at that time, there was nothing much in the way of organised lessons because we hadn't been integrated with the school as such. The teachers did quite a good job, they took us out for nature rambles in the countryside and I enjoyed it. I think most of us did because there were no actual lessons. Accommodation was found in a little hall in High Brooms and a small group started temporary lessons reading and one of the teachers managed to scrounge a film projector so we saw one or two educational films. Eventually we were integrated with the High Brooms Central School and we had our own classes but we didn't mix with the local children. The evacuees had their own teachers from home and their own classrooms.'

Don Crisp living with his sister in a village near Deal remembers:

'School was pretty fragmentary at that time because we were settling down. We were in a school in Deal and we had a section of it. I don't think the education authorities in Deal thought it would be a terribly good idea for the cockney kids to mix too much with the local boys and girls, so we were separated to a certain extent, at class times anyway.

'Playtimes were rumbustious affairs and no doubt there were little gang fights between the locals and the boys and girls from up the smoke.'

Evelyn Cundy, a teacher, remembers the difficulties of getting adequate school buildings:

'We spent the first few months in a series of non-conformist chapels. First of all we went to Bethel, then we went to Zion. Zion was right in the middle of the village, it was larger than Bethel. The minister's name was Bassett, so we used to call them Zion Bassett and Bethel Bassett. In Zion Bassett we were allowed to use the little rooms on the ground floor that were administrative rooms, little boxes that weren't much good for classes. We were not allowed to use the body of the church.

'There was, however, a big gallery like a theatre up above, so the main proportion of the children were up in this gallery from both Bethersden and Smarden. At one stage the buzz went around that a party was coming to inspect Zion to see if it was suitable. We were trying very hard to be moved. The day came and three or four people, including the acting headmistress came into the main church downstairs, while we were all busy teaching above. I thought I could do my bit to see if we could get moved, I could see fairly easily over the edge and watched the group obviously talking about this. Then they moved away, well away from just under us and I had a very unfortunate accident with my blackboard: it dropped and it made the most appalling clatter. I remember I was absolutely horrified. I had made sure they were out of the way before it dropped. I didn't tell anybody that it

Barbara Letchford's suitcase and teddy bear, which were evacuated with her to Canterbury in 1939. (B. Letchford)

wasn't anything but an accident and we were able to move soon after, which was very fortunate. It must have been a relief for the village head-master, because for a couple of afternoons in the week he had let us use his school very much at his own inconvenience, which was noble of him. We moved into Gilletts, a large house right in the middle of the village and we took that over completely as a school and were there until we were more or less bombed out.'

Call up of men at the beginning of the war meant that many schools lost their male staff. Women were called in to replace their male colleagues which in boys only schools was almost unheard of at that time. The Simon Langton Boys School in Canterbury was one school which lost male teachers during the call up and Mary Smith joined the staff. She remembers the demand for women to fill in where they could:

'I'd been educated at the Simon Langton Girls School and knew the area well so the Headmaster was pleased to take me on. Originally I was meant to stay about six weeks as they thought the war would be quite short, but I stayed twenty-eight years in all. The boys were surprisingly good, I thought they might be difficult and the headmaster thought so too, but they cer-tainly weren't. They were very nice most of them, very humorous and friendly. Many of them were country boys with wholesome interests. Some old chap congratulated me once on tackling those great fellows and of course they weren't a bit like that, they were large but they were quite friendly when you got to know them well.'

The first nine months of the war were relatively quiet with the result that many evacuees drifted home. However, in May 1940, after the British and Allied Troops were rescued from the advancing German Army at Dunkirk, the threat of an invasion cast a shadow over Britain, especially over Kent. Emergency evacuation plans were implemented to remove children to safer parts of the country and thousands of school children were rapidly escorted from the county.

Joan Small, evacuated from Clarendon House School in Ramsgate, remembers:

'I was told at school about three days before we were evacuated and given some advice about food and drink. We were told there wouldn't be much to drink and advised to get dried apricots. I had to search the shops.'

Eileen Dykes recalls how her school, the Barton Road School for Girls in Dover, reacted to the news:

'The teachers sent us all home with slips asking if our parents would like us to be evacuated. As I was an only child my mother said, "No I'm not letting you go," which upset me a great deal, because nearly all my friends were going. Anyhow it wasn't to be and I remember going with my dad to the Priory Station on a Sunday morning, where they were all assembled. Seeing them with their little labels and bags, some of them only had carrier bags, I felt awful and very sad and we saw them get on the train. There were no parents down there, they had obviously been told not to go. We went up the Priory steps to watch the train steam out and we came home and had Sunday dinner and I went off to Sunday School. There were about four children there and the Superintendent said that Sunday School would be shut from that day until people came back or until the end of the war. It was very, very quiet in Dover, there were no schools at all, everywhere was shut.'

Dover Grammar School girl, Beryl Mason, remembers leaving the town. She was thirteen years old at the time:

'I was so ashamed because my mother came to the station to see me off. She knew she was very ill and wouldn't see me again, she didn't live for very long. That was the last time I saw her.'

She was billeted as were many children from Kent, near Newport in South Wales in a small village, sharing a single bed with another evacuee. She asked her new hosts for an apple from a dish and they looked at her very strangely as obviously they were scarce in that part of the country.

Mary Smith at Simon Langton School for Boys in Canterbury, remembers this stage of evacuation:

'Some of the city boys went away for a time but gradually they drifted back. Most of the country boys stayed and used to go into school, although we were only allowed to have so many on the premises at one time. The country boys hated the idea of being evacuated, they were much happier

Lilian Parkes, pictured outside her home in Aylesford, survived the onslaught of sixteen evacuees from London.　(L. Parkes)

enjoying it all, if you can use such an expression, around here there was so much happening and they used to bring me things they'd found, pieces of perspex and bullets.'

The first bombs landed in Britain near Canterbury on 9th May 1940, which together with the Dunkirk evacuation and the Battle of Britain in the same year put the county firmly in the battle zone. Many schools were vulnerable to air attack by being near sites that were strategically important. The Maidstone Grammar School for Girls was one such school, as Doris Ayres point out, being near to Detling and between two railways.

Beryl Moore was a pupil in Gillingham during the Battle of Britain and remembers:

'A German plane came over machine gunning and one of the windows came in whilst the teacher was reading to us. Everyone was very scared with lots of screaming going on. We were just marched out to the shelter but it was frightening at the time.'

Bessie Newton was a fourteen-year-old Dover schoolgirl, whose father worked on the Pier. He had seen first hand the beginning of the Dunkirk evacuation and realised that the evacuation of the town's children would follow shortly. Bessie remembers:

'We didn't know until the Friday that we were going and we went on Sunday. I don't think we realised the full significance then of the horrible experience it was, we had no idea where we were being sent to, we were just put on the train and the end was an unknown destination.'

Joan Small from Ramsgate was evacuated from Clarendon House Grammar School to Staffordshire. She was rather more optimistic:

'I was fifteen, so more or less fully grown, and to us it was a big adventure. There were soldiers on one platform in Ramsgate who had just come off the boat from Dunkirk, who were being sent inland, as we children were going out on the other. The evening before we were evacuated, I remember walking along Ramsgate seafront and seeing all the soldiers coming in on the coaches. When we were actually told we were going to Staffordshire, we were horrified, because to us it said The Potteries, it was the only thing we could think of. We expected to end up in some smokey town somewhere, but of course, Stafford was a lovely market town in those days.'

Bessie Newton remembers her arrival at a small village called Caerleon and the advantages and disadvantages of being away from home.

'We arrived quite late in the evening and were taken to a hall. Another girl has told me since that we were then taken to a playground and examined for nits. I think that was because of all the publicity they had heard of the London children, some of whom were not exactly clean when they arrived. I don't think they were quite prepared for us at all. Unless you were very well off in those days you didn't have holidays, so you were never away from your parents. Mine was a very matriarchal home too so I missed my mother particularly, and also I was separated from my brother and sister. On the first night I refused to stay at a funny little cottage on the river bank, and I went back with my suitcase much to the horror of the mistresses who thought they had us all settled. Then I went into a house which was very upper class really and they were wonderful, I just had a wonderful time. I think really it was mainly to do with the companionship that came out of it. You made very close friends because you must remember that Dover County School in those days took pupils from all the little villages around as well as Deal and Sandwich, and when you said goodbye to someone after school, you didn't see them in the evening, or at the weekend, whereas there we made very close groups of friends and I am still in touch with them all today.'

Joan Small echoes Bessie's thoughts:

'That's exactly right, the fact that the girls at school were separated after school hours, one of my best friends lived in Birchington for instance and once we were evacuated she was actually living right next door. I was an only child and I found myself in a household where there was a boy who had just started teaching and two grammar school boys lived next door. It was a ready-made social life and we had a very thriving Green and Brown Club which was one of the important things in our lives in Stafford. Green and Brown for Clarendon House and Chatham House, the boys school also evacuated from Ramsgate. We used to meet once a week, I think that is where we all learned to dance. We had a very good band and all sorts of outings. We had a thriving drama group too which was something I hadn't been interested in at home particularly.'

Betty Harden, a pupil at Ashford County Grammar School, was evacuated in September 1940 to Oxford. The pupils had no idea where they were actually going and had been given a card already addressed to send as soon as they arrived. They were lucky enough to be billeted at a Priory in Burford, the home of Sir Archibald Southby who was MP for Epsom. Betty describes the accommodation:

'We had been quite a large family and rather poor and when we got to the Priory we found it was a very large place with its own chapel attached to it. We were given mostly bedrooms for two with hot and cold water, we had two bathrooms, it was very palatial. An old Elizabethan Ballroom with a long Gallery was our sitting room. We had the maids and the butlers sitting room for our dining room and the teacher had a lovely large bedroom with pink sheets, a thing unheard of in those days. A river ran through the grounds and we had a large boat which we were allowed to use and also a canoe, but we had to have supervision for that. The boathouse was an old Roman bath. We also had tennis courts which we could use whenever we liked.'

The girls from Ashford Grammar School went to Burford Grammar School which they found very old fashioned and indeed the inhabitants of Burford were shocked by the rather forward girls from Ashford who wore navy knickers and white blouses for gym.

Betty's experience of bombing in Kent helped her endure spending whole nights in the shelters while the bombing was going on over the Midlands and Coventry during the Battle of Britain. The Ashford girls took very little notice of the sirens because they were used to bombs, but the Head Mistress of Burford crawled around the school on all fours wearing her tin hat when the siren went.

Many children old enough to realise why they had been evacuated, feared for their parents' safety. Joan Small, evacuated to Staffordshire — an area which, compared with Kent, had hardly been touched by the effects of war — felt her parents in Ramsgate did not realise the rest of England was more peaceful.

'When you got letters from home, that's when you used to worry or you might get to school and someone would say, "Do you know there was a raid last night?" Then you worried.

'On a couple of occasions my parents did ring through to say they were all right and perhaps we didn't realise that anything could have been wrong but they had a raid and thought we might be worried.'

Many of Kent's school children remained scattered throughout the land for the duration of the war and whilst the memories we have gathered have been, in the main, happy ones, Bessie Newton reminds us:

'Whilst I was fortunate, many, many people were not. They had the most atrocious conditions when, for example, they were not allowed indoors in the day time, they were not well fed maybe, sleeping two to a single bed and so on. It wasn't good for lots and lots of people.'

Chapter V
LEND A HAND ON THE LAND

Throughout the war appeals were made for people to 'Lend A Hand On The Land' and thousands of volunteers came forward to replace some of the labour that the farmers had lost in the call-up. Food production was dramatically stepped up during the war years in an attempt to make the country self sufficient, as importing goods by sea was difficult and dangerous.

One of the most useful temporary workforces that came to the aid of the farmer in wartime was the Women's Land Army. The Land Army was reborn in June 1939, after its service in World War I, when a register was compiled of women willing to give up their non-essential jobs to work on the land if war came. The scheme was administered by women, and was headed by Lady Trudi Denman from her country home, Balcombe Place, in Sussex. The aim was to attract girls from factories, shops and offices who had always wanted an open air job.

One of the many Land Army recruits who ended up working in Kent was Dorothy Barton, who was aged nineteen and commuted to London where she worked in a Navy outfitters shop as a typist and book-keeper.

She recalls:

'It was while I was walking around in my lunch time that I noticed a recruiting office for the Land Army and went in and volunteered straight away. I wasn't really attracted to it but I couldn't think of anything else to do. I didn't want to go in the Army and salute everybody, the thought of saluting people horrified me for some reason, so when I saw the recruiting office for the Land Army, I signed on straight away. I had to go home and tell my parents and by the time I was half way home on the train I wondered if perhaps I had made a mistake. While we were having tea, I casually dropped into the conversation that I had just signed on for the Land Army and my Dad said, "You can just go and sign off again as fast as you like!"

'Of course I didn't, I let it stand and they got used to the idea of me going away from home. I would have been called up the following year because they started calling up women then, but I wanted to do something that I thought I would like to do instead of having to do what I was told to do, so that's why I chose the Land Army. They asked me at the interview what I knew about farm work — which was absolutely nothing — and could I drive a car and one or two other questions, but that was all.

Joan Chinery, land girl, in the milking
parlour of Manor Farm, Fairseat.

(J. Chinery)

'Then they said they desperately needed milkers to take the place of the
young men who were going into the Army and would I like to do that? I
didn't see why not so I said yes I would and they put me down as a milker.'

Although some girls were attracted to the Land Army because it had none of
the tiresome military disciplines of the other forces, others joined to pursue a
genuine desire to work in farming, like Joan Chinery from Fairseat, who joined
the Land Army in 1940 after working at Bon Marche in Gravesend.

'My father's family were farmers, my father was a butcher and I'd always
loved animals and thought I'd love to work out in the open. I don't know
why, but we had to sign on at Gravesend Police Station. I went there and
said to all the chaps sitting in the office, the policemen that is, "I want to
join the Women's Land Army." It seems I was the first person to volunteer
in Gravesend and one of them turned round to the other chaps and said,
"We've got someone here to grow our spuds for us." I replied, "You'll be
jolly glad of the Land Army when the war is over."'

It took some time for the Women's Land Army to be taken more seriously, but
perhaps part of the reason why people found it amusing was that many of the
girls who joined were city girls, more used to commuting to work by train,
wearing smart outfits and being cooped up in an office, shop or factory all day.
For these girls, the Land Army was a completely new way of life as Marion
Hinkley from Tenterden remembers:

'To start with we were all in our usual various jobs in offices or whatever line of work we were in and the Government said that all girls and women of a certain age had to find some job in the national service. They had the ATS and they had the WAAFs and they had the WRENs and then along came the poor sister — they called it the Cinderella of the services — the Land Army. Many of the land girls came from towns, they were shop girls, office girls and from various other jobs; I was actually in catering. It was a completely different way of life for them when they came down. Some went into milking, others to general farming and some would specialise. Some were taught to plough, some did forestry, they even did hedging and ditching and then some looked after sheep. It was very general — but it was very hard work, very long hours and out in all weathers.'

Because they were engaged in essential war work, the members of the Women's Land Army were kitted out in a distinctive, practical uniform. Dorothy Barton remembers hers arriving in the post . . .

'The uniform arrived in several large parcels and it all took a long time. The working uniform was quite smart, a bib and brace overalls with a matching three-quarter length jacket, leather lace-up boots and knee length socks. Then we had wellingtons with thick stockings inside, a short sleeve cream Aertex shirt and a long sleeve cotton shirt. We were also given a pork pie hat, a green V-neck pullover and a pair of brown velveteen breeches cut far too wide at the top, so they drooped over the knees, very wide and baggy, so I altered mine to fit a bit better.'

The state did not provide everything. The girls had to surrender some of their clothing coupons in exchange for the uniform, and they also had to supply their own underwear and nightwear. The uniform was very popular among its wearers, including Joan Chinery who was really proud of it.

The wide-brimmed soft hat worn by the Land Army girls became a trademark and it could be adapted to any shape that best suited its wearer. However the hat was not meant for wearing while working on the farm, contrary to some of the pictures that were published at the time, as Dorothy Barton remembers:

'You'd get pictures of girls out in the fields with their hats on but we never wore our hats in the fields, they were for walking out when we always wore uniform — we were very rarely in civvies.'

Having been kitted out in uniform, the next step in a land girl's career was to undergo some form of training, and it was usually at this stage that any preconceived illusions about the country life were shattered, as Dorothy Barton describes:

'I went to a training farm with a hostel not far from Sevenoaks. We went for a month to be trained as milkers. It was really hard work. We got up about four or half past four in the morning and went along and had bread and jam

Marion Hinkley driving a milk float in Sevenoaks early in the war. (M. Hinkley)

and a cup of tea. Then we went to the farm where they had about eighty cows. First of all we were shown how to clean a cow, scrape all the muck off it and wash its udders, and we watched the cows being milked a couple of times. Then we were given a bucket and a three legged stool, made to put on a white coat and hat and told to get on with it. Well, I sat down at mine, grabbed hold of the teats and started milking. I got some milk and I was really thrilled, "I thought I'm a milker", but after about a pint of milk there was nothing. It just stopped and I sat there for ages and ages pulling away, changing the combination of teats to see if that would have any effect. I began to worry that I'd done the cow some damage as the milk wasn't coming through. By this time, my hands were really frozen into position. I don't think they've ever ached so much, but eventually one of the senior girls stopped beside me, looked in my bucket and said, "Good girl, you've got some — now let me have a go."

'I didn't like to say it wasn't working. Still she sat down, thumped the cow on the side and said, "Let it go you something or other" (I won't repeat the exact word), and the bucket immediately filled with frothy milk; she laughed and explained that the cows quite often hold back their milk when they don't know the milker and that it would be alright next time or the time after.

'They used that as a little joke on the rookies, not telling us in advance that this might happen. I was really worried at first, but in the afternoon and on the next day it was alright and I was milking.

'After we finished milking, we had breakfast then back to the farm again when half of us cleaned out the sheds, cleared out the muck and cleaned the stalls, while the other half went into the dairy, sterilised the milk and bottled it. Then we returned to the hostel for lunch. We had a long lunch hour, most of us were exhausted, so we laid down on our beds for half an hour. In the afternoon, we went back and started all over again. In that whole month I had two half days off, we worked ten or twelve days without any break whatever and for that every week I got a postal order for 8/- (40p).

'We worked about twelve hours a day in that training school, had an evening meal and a bath and just fell into bed and up again about four o'clock the next morning — so we didn't do anything, couldn't spend the money on anything except on going home on our two half days.'

Marion Hinkley from Tenterden was considered too small to be suitable for the WAAF and started her Land Army career in Beckenham, wobbling around on a tricycle delivering milk, but eventually she too found herself getting to grips with cows when she went to train on a farm near Sevenoaks and echoes Dorothy Barton's experiences:

'We had to get up at four in the morning to start work, roughly about half past five to six. We learned milking, bottling and all the things one does to produce milk. Of course, at first you struggle like anything and no milk comes out at all.'

Joan Chinery was another Land Army milkmaid, but she didn't have the luxury of training, for her it was straight in at the deep end.

'I had none, I just went there and I was taught, I just took to it and I loved it. It was a wonderful job, smashing. The farmer's nephew was in the cowshed with me and he taught me all I know about cows. He was a farmer's son and he was marvellous. All I know about cows, Alf taught me.'

The Women's Land Army members were expected to be able to work just as hard and just as long as any burly male farm labourer, and they undertook a very wide variety of different tasks. Mary O'Connolly was a Londoner on holiday hop picking from her work as a tailoress in a London factory, when war was declared. She decided to stay on in a billet in Marden, and soon became another Land Army recruit:

'Into Maidstone, into Union Street and fill in the form, pass an exam, then a medical of course, and because I was billeted in Kent, I could find my own farmer, I wasn't just put on to someone. I thought the nearer the better so I was the land girl for Mr Stanley in Marden. He owned the garage and a farm out the back. I worked for him for six months and then because it was only

Some of the young women under the care of Miss Winifred Parrish, Matron of the Women's Land Army Hostel at Lenham. (D. Barton)

a small farm with the majority of the work catering for the garage and repairs, I went on to work for Mr Alan Firmin of Wares Farm, Linton, near Maidstone. I went as a tractor driver but I didn't do much tractor driving because they already had someone — and they were a bit funny those men — so I did all the fruit picking. Mr Firmin bought an orchard over at Frittenden and I had the job of driving the pony and trap all the way to Frittenden and at the end of the day, loaded up with plums I drove all the way back to Linton.

'I learned to ride a motorbike, a twin American Harley Davidson, a self-starter and a great big heavy machine and I went riding around with my hat flapping. Then I started driving a lorry, an artic. First of all it was an old Army Bedford which I took loaded with apples to Covent Garden in the blackout, the headlight was just a little cross and I was only eighteen and weighed six and a half stone. Being a land girl you didn't have to unload, the porters unloaded for you. Then the next day you'd have half a day off.

'I did other jobs too, tree washing three times a year, pruning which I've done with snow on the ground and while it was snowing, apple picking, apple wrapping and apple packing, plum picking, all fruit in fact, because my governor bought orchards. The dirtiest work was muck spreading which we did do at Linton, which if you are on your own is boring.'

Luckily Mary usually had her friend Elsie working with her, which made the time pass more quickly. Marion Hinkley had to do without female company when she finished her training and began work.

'I was eventually engaged to look after a small herd of cows at Tenterden and I was found a billet. I was the only girl on the farm and I was there first thing in the morning. There was no electricity so I lit the oil lamps then washed the cows in cold water and sat down to the milking.

'The very first cow I sat under kicked over my bucket which wasn't, of course, very encouraging. After milking, I fed the cows and if it was fine weather, let them out, then I had to dung out the cow-shed, which was jolly hard work, with a wheelbarrow and a fork wheeling it out on a sort of gang-plank to the dung heap. After that I would do general farming, hop training, fruit picking, potato picking, worzel cutting and in the summer there was the usual haymaking and harvesting.'

Dorothy Barton also helped with the harvest:

'Mr B taught me to load waggons, interlocking the sheaves of corn so they didn't fall off. I helped him with the building of the haystacks and corn-stacks. Once you get the rhythm and you were shown the right way to hoist up a sheaf of corn on the end of a pitchfork, then you could do it most of the day.'

Faced with a shortage of labour, together with demands from the Ministry of Agriculture to step up their production, farmers were keen to make use of whatever labour was available, and most welcomed the land girls to their farms.

Much depended on the type of work required in the opinion of Tom Miller, a fruit grower from Eastry, as he explains:

'A land girl was not nearly as good as a man. For example, in winter I taught them how to prune trees but they only managed twelve rows in the whole winter while two men pruned all the rest of the farm.'

Norman Steed of Grove, near Canterbury, had a farm near Manston during the war, and he had no reservations about using land girls, remembering how good they had been in World War I:

'I had several land girls in the course of time, they were all local girls but they had joined the Land Army and were kitted out in the uniform. One just puts a person to work, shows them what to do and hopes that they will do it to the best of their ability, which they did. They were very good workers.'

The farmers may have welcomed the extra help, but how did the remaining male farm labourers view their new colleagues from the Land Army? Gwen Lonsdale from Maidstone recollects:

'They didn't think we would be able to do the work.' But Marion Hinkley observed a change in attitude:

'They just took the mickey at first, but when they saw we knuckled down, because the majority of girls did, they changed their minds. Many girls stayed on the land for the duration of the war and in the end a lot of them married into the local villages or towns.'

Dorothy Barton, second from the left, enjoying a break with other land girls in Torquay.
(D. Barton)

The recruitment posters and press photographs of the Women's Land Army showed smiling, beautifully turned out girls carrying sheaves of corn, or feeding lambs in the spring sunshine. For some of the land girls, the country life really did live up to the publicity. At the farm where Joan Chinery worked the Jersey herd was homebred.

'It was like that really, because here at Fairseat we kept most of our heifer calves and I used to rear them. They were lovely. I put milk in a bucket, put my fingers in the bucket and they used to suck my fingers to start with. Then they got used to it and started to drink themselves. It was a grand life.'

Many farmers soon realised that the land girls got on well with animals and put them to work caring for livestock. Joan Chinery adored working with her cows . . . but after eighteen months decided she wanted a change although this was short-lived:

'I went to Mr Whitebread's at Wainscott, a fruit farm and he sent me over to his Higham Farm where I worked the horses. I helped with the fruit picking and that sort of thing, but the Land Army was appealing for milkers, so as I'd done that I thought I ought to go back to a dairy farm and went to one in

Chattenden, which is a housing estate now. There I hand-milked and at first you had a job to get a cupful of milk, but after a while it came naturally. I was there seven years hand-milking and that was lovely!'

Dorothy Barton was also given the chance to work with cows, but things did not always go according to plan, especially since some farmers were still dubious about the land girls' ability to do farm work . . .

'I was sent to a private farm quite a long way away and I was very pleased with myself. I arrived at the farm and it took me a long time to get there. I arrived about teatime one Saturday. I knocked on the door and the farmer answered, took one look at me and said, "Oh no dear, I'm sorry, I wanted a bigger, stronger girl than you. It's fairly heavy work round here, I don't think you'll be big enough." He would have sent me back straight away but his wife came out and said something about not sending me home without any tea so I went in and had some tea and stayed the night.

'I got up early next morning and they asked me if I would mind getting the cows in and I thought, well I can do that, so off I went to the field where these cows were — an absolute quagmire, liquid mud and liquid cow manure, all mixed up together. When I went to call them, the cows didn't know me so they walked away and I hurried to get behind them so I could drive them in and while I was rushing along, I put my foot in a hole and I fell face down, flat on the ground in all that mess. I thought to hell with the cows, picked myself up and went back to the farmhouse. The farmer's wife wouldn't let me in, of course — well, who would? She made me go to a nearby chicken house, take off all my clothes, my brand new Land Army uniform, which she dropped into a bath of cold water, gave me a blanket which I wrapped around myself and it took me the best part of the day to get myself clean, especially my hair. I went home at tea time feeling absolutely embarrassed and disgraced.

'On Monday morning I rang the Land Army to tell them. I thought I'd get the sack but they were very good and said lots of farmers thought girls weren't strong enough and when I told them about falling in the mess they fell about laughing.'

Mechanisation was only just beginning to affect Kent farms during wartime, and much work was still extremely labour intensive, including fruit picking, harvesting and milking. Horses were widely used, and again it fell to the land girls to work with them, even though some had little or no experience. Unlike a tractor, a horse has a mind of its own, as many found out to their cost. Dorothy Barton was living in a hostel for land girls in Lenham when she first had to work with horses . . .

'I was given a job on a farm just out on the edge of the village and the first Monday morning I was told to go and find Mr B as I was to work with him. He was a lovely old man and with him was one of the biggest horses I had

Light refreshments during harvesting for Joan Chinery. (J. Chinery)

The Land Girl magazine appeared monthly, price 3d (1½p) encouraging women to continue their hard work — 'Determine that, having put your hand to the plough, you will not turn back until victory is won'. (J. Chinery)

ever seen. I discovered I was to work with horses. There were two horses on the farm and Mr B was in charge. I did everything with horses, it was a wonderful job, wonderful.

'The first Monday was a disaster. I had to lead the horse up and down between rows of cabbages and the horse was attached to a sort of frame with several hoes on it so that we could hoe two or three rows at a time. I had to lead the horse while Mr B was at the back guiding the "shim", as it was called.

'There I was with this massive horse whose head was way above my shoulders, I'd never been near a horse before so I was terrified of it. Nevertheless, I got hold of his bridle and started to walk up the field. After a few minutes he realised I had no control over him so he took off, quite fast, with me dangling and Mr B calling out rude things from the rear.

'By the time he'd got the horse to stop, instead of hoeing between them, we'd ploughed up several rows. Mr B made me go and put them all back after he'd nagged me. Well for the rest of the day things worked out a bit better and I finally got the hang of leading the horse.

'After lunch Mr B said as I'd done so well, forgetting the first ten minutes, he'd show me how to turn a horse at the end of a row so that he didn't tread on the chains and trip himself up; I did this and got on very well. After about a quarter of an hour doing this up and down the row turning him by myself with Mr B yelling, "Watch his feet," well I was watching Tinker's feet but I forget to watch my own. As the horse stepped sideways he put his great hoof on my foot which just sank into the ground with this massive shire horse standing on it. Fortunately the ground was soft but when I shrieked the horse just stood there because he thought I wanted him to stop.

'I sat down and cried because I really thought my foot was smashed, but Mr B came and just lifted Tinker's hoof up and I lifted my foot out of the hole in the ground. My foot was actually only badly bruised and had to be strapped up for several days, but after that I watched my feet as well as Tinker's.'

Dorothy came into contact with horses again later on in the war at another farm . . .

'Once I had to look after a sick horse, I spent four or five weeks doing nothing else but dosing this animal with drenches, rubbing his legs with embrocation and making him walk or trying to walk, the poor old thing was so ill he couldn't walk. Eventually I got him to walk and led him to the duck pond where he had to stand every day, but old Jack didn't like the cold water on his inflamed legs. After I'd led him into the pond I turned to walk back to the bank but he beat me to it every time. In the end, I had to stand in the pond for a quarter of an hour twice a day to make sure Jack stayed there. Finally he got well and fully recovered so that was another job finished and I was back at the hostel again.'

Kent's land girls worked long and hard but they knew how to enjoy themselves, as Mick Johns who lived at Pembury explains:

'There used to be a field opposite us and during the war we had the land girls coming in right left and centre. They were on all the farms around us. They were a happy old lot. There were Scots lasses, some from Yorkshire, all over the country they came from. They had a horse drawn cutter for the corn, stacking it up with hand stacks, chucking it onto the horse and cart. They were a merry lot they were. They used to like their little old drinks as well at times, in the local pubs at night, spending their well-earned money. They were a really good lot.'

There were many thousands of soldiers stationed in Kent and the troops often had entertainment laid on to help boost morale, and land girls were sometimes able to join in. Land girl Joan Chinery from Fairseat was working on a farm in Chattenden, right next to a military barracks:

'There was no entertainment or anything put on for the land girls and I was so lucky, as next door to the farm was a Royal Marine Camp and their commanding officer Major Attwood mentioned that we girls never had any

Memorabilia from Joan Chinery's days as a land girl. The Manual with plenty of advice for upholding the Land Army's motto 'Stick To It', with Joan's proficiency medals and membership card. (J. Chinery)

enjoyment and invited us to their ENSA concerts. I said that would be lovely but told him there was another land girl working with me. He said bring her along so we used to go to their ENSA dances and films and it did make a great difference. We had a very good time and they had a dance once a month. It was a commando camp and they used to have the young fellows in for commando training.'

The local military personnel soon discovered that Mary O'Connolly had valuable musical talents which they put to good use . . .

'The troops came to Marden and asked me to join their band with the piano accordion and I did. We had a band for three years and every Saturday night we played in the Memorial Hall. It was 1/6d (7½p) to go in and during the interval when they had tea and biscuits, I would don my roller skates and do a roller dance exhibition. So after that we were hired out to different villages on Saturday nights.

'We lived next door to the pub, The Unicorn Hotel, and because the war was on and everyone was so sad, they'd ask me to play the squeeze box at the darts matches. It wasn't really a squeeze box but a 180 Bass Giraldo. I'd play all the London songs and everyone felt so happy they forgot the war because you were giving them a little entertainment.'

The Land Army hostel at Lenham, where Dorothy Barton lived, was home for around forty land girls, who worked on any farm in the area that needed them.

84

Although they worked long hours, the girls still found time for socialising, and many of them went out with local boys. But there was no danger of the girls compromising their moral standards, as the Matron of the hostel became their self-appointed guardian:

'She was an absolutely wonderful person, any land girl will know Miss Winifred Parrish, she looked after us as if we were her own daughters. She made us laugh sometimes because when we first had a full complement of girls, she called us all together and told us she had decided that as naturally we would have boyfriends and callers at the house and she didn't mind us having them, they would have to come to the house to collect us. We were not to meet them on street corners. She arranged a row of chairs in the hall for the young men to sit on while they were waiting and anyone who came to call for a girl had to give a potted history while he was waiting. She would yell out the name of the girl and all the others used to peer over the banisters to look at the date sitting in the hall. Funnily enough, the young men didn't seem to mind this, they all liked Matron very much indeed.

'Because few of us had watches, Matron decided she would ring a bell just before ten o'clock so we could go back to the hostel, the idea being that we should be in by then because we were up early in the morning. Well we couldn't hear this little bell so she said she'd find something we could hear. The next night she had a great big iron frying pan and a wooden spoon and stood outside the door of the hostel banging away at this thing and you could hear it way outside the limits of the village. When we heard it we used to scatter up the road so as to be in before ten.'

Although there was not such a good choice of entertainment in the countryside as there was in the towns of Kent, there were many dances held during the war years, and with so many troops in the area, the girls were never short of partners as Dorothy Barton recounts:

'We would get invitations from Army camps in the area and Matron insisted that they sent transport for us so we would all go together and come back together. We had to leave the dances at eleven o'clock to be back by half-past, this was usually an extension for Saturday dances. The Army transport would call for us in the early evening and any of the local girls who wanted could go to the hostel and get picked up at the same time and we'd go to the dance. About eleven o'clock, the MC would yell out "Land Army Transport here", and we'd have to leave the floor and come home. Some of the local girls came with us too if we were far away, but sometimes they stayed on and came back by bus or with boyfriends or whatever, but we land girls had to leave by 11 pm.'

The troops and Land Army gave many of Kent's sleepy villages a new lease of life. There were a number of Land Army girls based around the Tenterden area, along with the build-up of troops, so the usually quiet little town really came to life during the war years . . .

Joan Chinery's armlet — half a diamond was sewn on after every six month's of satisfactory service. (J. Chinery)

Vera Holdstock remembers:

'There were a lot of dances and parties and people in the pubs. First of all the Army was stationed in Tenterden and later the American Air Force just outside and with the young farmers, men and women, Tenterden was a very lively place during the war.'

Land girl Marion Hinkley, also living in Tenterden, took advantage of the opportunity for a weekend break:

'Somebody arranged little hops, dances for the forces once a week, so you could go there. It cost 6d (2½p) to go for a very good evening's entertainment and mixing. But apart from that, you were far too tired. You got up at six and you worked, physical hard work, till night-time and you were only too glad to go home, wash, change, have a meal and hop into bed and before you knew where you were, it was the morning.'

The Women's Land Army in Kent faced frontline conditions during the war, but farm life still had to continue despite enemy activity, as the work of the Land Army was vital for the country's war effort in providing much needed food supplies. The Germans certainly did not make the Land Army's job any easier, as Joan Chinery recalls:

'I know one night we'd just started milking and there was a terrible raid. We could hear the schrapnel pinging down on the galvanised roof. We couldn't open the doors to let the cows out after the milking because of showing a light so we sat there for ages waiting for the raid to finish. Well it didn't. There were bombers going up towards London and searchlights and the ack-ack were on. In the end we put the lights out and groped between the cows to let them out. This was about ten o'clock at night.'

During the Battle of Britain in the late summer of 1940, Kent's harvest was brought in as dogfights between the RAF and Luftwaffe went on overhead. Some farmers dug trenches for their workers to shelter in if the activity above

86

grew too intense, but often farm workers, including the Women's Land Army, carried on with their work regardless of the danger. Dorothy Barton recalls that it was not always possible to take proper safety precautions while working:

'We were supposed to wear helmets. We had steel helmets, not quite the same shape as the soldiers' helmets and a bit awkward to wear because when you bent down it tipped forward onto your nose, so generally we left them with our lunch tins under the hedge and of course, we needed them when the bombs and shrapnel were falling and they were always on the other side of the field, so in the end, we didn't bother to take them. We went without helmets and just hoped for the best.'

Unlike the regular armed services, the Women's Land Army provided no opportunities for promotion within its ranks. But to keep up their morale, Land Army Honorary Director, Lady Denman, sent letters to the girls every six months congratulating them on their work. There was also the opportunity for them to take proficiency certificates for different aspects of farm work, such as care of horses, or milking, as Joan Chinery experienced:

'For hand-milking I went to a farm near Maidstone and for machine-milking to a farm in Fairseat. There were farmers there and vets and they stood and watched you do your job and then the milk was tested to make sure there was no hair or anything from the cow in it.'

Regular forces could win medals for bravery and good service to their country and were entitled to a demob suit when they left the services. But the Women's Land Army had a more modest system of reward, as Marion Hinkley recalls:

'Well we ended up with an overcoat, a pair of trousers and a hat. When you'd been in the Land Army for six months you were given a half diamond to sew on to your armband. When you had been a land girl for four years, you were given a splendid new armband with your diamonds woven on it.'

The other main perk of the job for land girls was an entitlement to some extra food rations to keep them going, but these rations surprisingly did not always come from the farms the girls worked on as Joan Chinery explains:

'The only extra we got was cheese, twelve ounces a week. That was the only extra food and I don't know if this was a general thing but I used to get it in a tin from Australia. I kept one of those tins and it was years after the war when I said to my mother, "I'm going to open that to see what it is like," and it was beautiful. It must have been fifteen years after the war finished.'

Although the tangible perks of the Land Army were few, the young women who lent a hand on the land in Kent during the Second World War derived job satisfaction and sense of purpose as expressed by Joan Chinery:

'When I was hand-milking, I would sit there and perhaps get a bucketful of milk and think it's feeding somebody. You know I had that feeling, I felt I was doing something.'

Dick Body of Snargate reliving the memory of being in an Operational Base.   (R. Body)

Joyce Bishop, a member of Crayford Civil Defence, with her father, Harry Jones, a Company Sergeant of the 18th Dartford Battalion of the Home Guard.   (J. Bishop)

Borden Home Guard with Bert Lewis in the middle of the back row.   (R. Lewis)

88

Chapter VI
KENT'S LOCAL DEFENCE VOLUNTEERS

On the evening of Tuesday 14th May 1940 Anthony Eden, the Secretary of State for War, broadcast an appeal for volunteers to join a part-time local defence organisation designed to combat paratroop landings behind the main defence lines. British subjects, men between the ages of seventeen and sixty-five, were eligible to join the new force named the Local Defence Volunteers. Uniforms and arms were promised. Reasonable fitness and a knowledge of firearms were the only requirements with the appeal directed to those who lived in small towns, villages or country parishes.

Police stations all over Kent were immediately inundated with volunteers. At Cranbrook and Gillingham, men were turning up to sign on even before Anthony Eden had finished speaking. At Folkestone, men were still queuing up at midnight and it is estimated that 10,000 volunteers enrolled in the first twenty-four hours. Among them was Colin Cuthbert, from Margate:

'I joined the Home Guard when the announcement was made on the radio asking for all able-bodied young men and old men and anybody else, to take up arms to report to the local police station and I was down there in about thirty minutes. I hoped I was one of the first to enrol.'

The following day, 15th May, Brigadier-General Franklin was asked to organise the LDV and its chain of command in Kent. Over the next two days, 3,500 rifles were delivered to Headquarters in Maidstone, Ashford and Canterbury, to be distributed to selected recruits. By 10.30 in the evening on 18th May, four days after Anthony Eden had first broadcast his appeal for volunteers, more than 1,000 armed men were on duty throughout Kent.

Despite this stirring start for a tiny minority of recruits, the LDV faced enormous problems in getting adequate supplies of weapons and equipment. One of Tenterden's first recruits was George Freeland . . .

'When Anthony Eden made the broadcast appealing for help and we had to go to the police station and register, which I did, we had armbands marked "LDV, and no firearms at all. In fact we were told to use sticks or poles to defend ourselves, quite impossible.'

Bill Callan from Northfleet remembers his early days as a volunteer:

'I joined the Home Guard which was a bit of a mixed bag of odds and bods, all types, we even had one chap who turned up on the first parade with his hat across his head like a pirate and his gaiters upside down. I think we had one machine gun and two rifles for the men on guard. There were about twenty of us and that is all we had. We went around and dug various trenches. We were to keep the pumping station protected from the Germans, which rather makes me laugh.'

On joining the LDV, new recruits did not receive any uniforms, those came later. It was a common sight in Kent to see newly formed units parading in civvies of varying degress of smartness, but Colin Cuthbert had great faith in his armband:

'All we had was an armband saying LDV, and that sort of made it legal. I got a feeling, mistakenly, that if you had one of those on, the Germans wouldn't shoot you.'

Although they were well armed later in the war initial training was with broom handles and sticks and many units were supplied with molotov cocktails or even pikes made out of lengths of gas piping with a bayonet fixed in the end. But the farmers and First World War veterans who volunteered could usually put their hands on a weapon of some kind. Colin Cuthbert recalls his first parade in part of Northdown Park in Cliftonville . . .

'There was a very cosmopolitan bunch of people of all ages and stages, doctors, brewers, shopkeepers, old men, young men like myself in that day, and the Superintendent of the Police was in charge of the parade and he asked everyone to fall in in threes, which I did for the first time in my life. We were told that the country was in a parlous state and that things were serious which we knew from what we had seen with our own eyes coming ashore down Margate Pier. We were going to try and do what we could so he asked had anybody got any guns or any armaments at all? To my surprise every man there dived his hand under his coat and produced relics from the First World War and an assortment of old guns. These were collected and that was the beginning.'

As the administrative wheels ground into action, weapons and supplies gradually began to reach the Local Defence Volunteers, including a number of rifles from America which were stored in a thick layer of yellow grease. Then it was just a matter of learning to use them. Bill Callan remembers a near miss in his family:

'My father was in the Home Guard, well all my uncles were in the Home Guard, albeit most of the time they only had a 12-bore shotgun, but latterly they did have rifles and my dad was the main anti-tank firer. He had a phosphorus bomb on the end of his and one Sunday on manoeuvres, instead of the bomb going off 200 yards away, it dropped out the end of the rifle and exploded, more or less, and burnt his shoes, but luckily he was okay.'

Certain groups of war workers were not allowed to join the regular LDV, but instead formed their own battalions in their work places. There were four so-called 'Utility Battalions' in Kent, the Kent Electrical, the Kent Bus, the GPO and the Southern Railway, whose membership in the end included Dick Rose of Folkestone, as he recounts:

'I tried to join the Local Defence Volunteers and I was sent back to the Sergeant and had my name removed and got severely told off, but eventually we did form our own "28 Battalion" of the Southern Railway Kent Home Guard.'

On joining the LDV, new recruits were asked four questions:

What is your occupation?
Are you familiar with firearms?
What military experience do you have? and
Are you prepared to serve away from home?

Joyce Bishop's father, who had been disabled in the First World War, was one of those who came forward to join the LDV. He became company clerk to D Company, and Joyce recorded all the details of the Dartford LDV in her diary:

'My father was in the 18th Battalion Home Guard and the Commanding Officer was Colonel Lord Dudley Gordon, who later became the Marquis of Aberdeen. When the LDV, as they were first called, were formed in Dartford, 200 volunteers gathered at the local police station within hours. Eventually 1,300 men were enrolled to serve the area and each night after work the men of D Company unit met for training sessions. This included drills, exercise, manoeuvres and shooting practice. Constant patrols were kept on the key areas in the Dartford marshes and on all the factories.'

As well as going out on military exercises and manoeuvres, the LDV had to learn to handle their weapons. As Colin Cuthbert recalls, the First World War veterans soon put their skills to good use teaching the younger members.

'The training was that the old soldiers showed us how to handle a gun. All sorts of people were in the Home Guard and I always remember one gentleman, a Mr Makepeace, who was a very nice man. He used to carry his gun like a farmer, under the armpit with the gun pointing to the ground in front of him.

'He used to walk around with this 303 and one day he accidentally pulled the trigger and he put a shot in the ground about eighteen inches from my foot. I felt the draught go up my trouser leg and I counted up to five and made sure my foot was still joined to me! However, everybody was helpful and very keen and enthusiastic to do something.'

Most of the LDVs had little or no previous experience of military procedures, so training was a priority as Martin Mason describes:

'The Home Guard used to drill and train and have a rifle drill. We used to go on firing ranges and learn to use various mortars and other equipment.'

Fred Lewis' LDV unit set about preparing itself to guard the aerodrome at Shorts Aircraft Factory in Rochester, but with such a motley selection of men and a shortage of equipment, Fred wondered if they would ever be capable of providing a credible fighting force.

'It was really laughable when you look back and they don't stretch a point by any means on Dad's Army when I compared it with my days in the Home Guard. We were taught originally how to load and unload and where to point your gun and safety precautions. We only had one or two guns in the unit but these did increase after a while and by the time we went into the trench to guard the aerodrome we all had a gun.

'We used to patrol the outside of the buildings at night, we were given a password for the night and then it was a question of "Halt, who goes there?" and if we didn't get the correct answer, well we were supposed to take action.'

On 3rd August 1940 the Kent LDV became affiliated to local infantry regiments such as the Queen's Own Royal West Kent Regiment and the East Kent Regiment known as the Buffs. This meant co-operation between the LDVs and the regular army both in training and combining forces in their areas to some extent. Harry Eede was a Battery Sergeant Major manning guns on the Kent coast near Folkestone and recalls training LDVs to take over from the regular army when the threat of invasion had diminished:

'We were told to train the Home Guard so that they could take over in a part-time capacity because the invasion scare was dying and we all got drafted away. If you were good enough you went in the field artillery and if you weren't good enough then you went to the infantry, unfortunately. We trained them on guns and of course it was a bit difficult because they were only part-time and they were tied up with various other things. Every now and again we would be in the middle of a gun drill and Mrs Brown would come over and ask where her husband was, then she would tell him to go home as his dinner was ready and he would have to leave. It was rather amusing but they were good men, a lot older than us at the time and they could have, in our opinion, taken our posts with the guns when we left and I think they would have done a good job.'

It was sometimes the case that when the regular army left the county for more urgent postings abroad, the Home Guard really were left as sole defenders of the area. More often they took on the task of filling in the gaps in the county's defences and for some of the young members, like Colin Cuthbert, this meant fitting in their duties round a hectic social life . . .

'We used to go to a dance which ended about eleven o'clock at night, then we used to go straight off from there to the Home Guard duty and we worked from mid-night to dawn, which sometimes in the winter was seven o'clock in the morning. We used to do a seven-hour stint on top of the cliffs and we were literally on the cliff tops. There was no mucking about, you were there to see things. We always thought there were a lot of troops behind us right up the line to back us, but (funnily enough, since I've read the history of the war) they weren't near us at all and I think we had been written off as expendable.'

On 23rd August 1940, on Churchill's insistence, the Local Defence Volunteers changed their name to the Home Guard. This was at the start of the Battle of Britain which proved to be a very busy time for the civil defence forces, with so much enemy activity in the skies over Kent. The bulk of the Home Guard's work continued to consist of guarding strategic sites, as Martin Mason from Dartford recalls:

'It was centred on local factories and places like power stations. It meant going to work during the day and then going on Home Guard duty in the evening.'

Shorts Aircraft factory in Rochester made Stirling Bombers, the first four-engined bomber to be made in the country, so it was an obvious target for the Germans.

On 15th August 1940 Shorts factory was dive-bombed by a formation of German Dornier bombers and a few volunteer soldiers armed with rifles were little use against the firepower of the Luftwaffe, as Fred Lewis recalls:

'The summer was a beautiful summer and the sky was very clear and I can remember now the sergeant saying, "There are bombers coming, they are diving, the bombs are actually coming down, take cover — get down." And so we all got down and sure enough we heard the explosion very much too close for comfort and then we got the blast from the bombs and we finished up, to my knowledge, with our heads between each others' legs and we were in complete disarray obviously.'

Many of the Home Guard recruits were too old to enlist in the regular forces, but it also served as a magnet for boys who were too young to be called up. It was a chance for them to do something positive for the war effort.
Eric Pearson from Tonbridge:

'We went on exercises. I remember the shooting rifle range at Castle Hill. We went up there and we used to go in the butts and mark the targets and I can remember Percy Nicholls, an elderly postman, saying, "Come on lads, it's your turn now," and giving us an old-fashioned Lee Enfield 303 to fire.'

Arthur Smith was another young recruit to the Home Guard. He had just left school and was working as a fitter's mate at the East Kent Road Car Company when he joined in Canterbury . . .

'I put my age up from fifteen to sixteen and I used to do duties at the Home Guard down in the mint yard. I think basically it was getting back at Hitler if

Some of the equipment provided for the Auxiliary Units to trap the enemy. From left to right: pull switch with attached trip wire, spool of trip wire, pressure switch, spool of trap wire, release switch, climping tool, time pencil and a charge made up with cordtex and a detonating fuse held in place with magnets. (R. Body)

ever he came over here. I wanted to be a soldier, I wanted to serve my country. They needed messenger boys because there was no communication. The Home Guard met at various public houses, then they would guard a specific thing like railway crossings, viaducts or power stations and so forth. The messenger boys' job was to keep contact from Headquarters to these various posts. This was done on our push bikes, just basic training of taking messages, writing messages down, but mostly you had to remember them in case you were ever caught, because during air raids it was always anticipated that Germans would land immediately afterwards so we had to be really on top of things as it were.'

The wide range of ages and abilities of the Home Guard members, combined with their acute lack of equipment in the early stages, meant that many people found it hard to take the Home Guard seriously. The volunteers usually managed to hold their heads up despite local opinion and made the best of a bad job using their own initiative to improvise with the facilities they had available, as Winifred Baker of St Mary's Platt explains:

'My husband was responsible for forming the first lot of LDVs, as they were then called. It was rather pathetic in a way, they went round getting volunteers and things from the farmers. They met every night and made Molotov cocktails. What they were made of I don't know, petrol I suppose, which we had in our garage. At that time there was a very well-known lady, Mrs Maxwell, who lived in the big house across the road. She gave us a three-sided cattle shed to give them some sort of protection at night-time, but it was very draughty. The boards didn't meet and I distinctly remember pasting layers of pages from magazines in the cracks to make it a little bit warmer for them. It was all rather Heath Robinson.'

Some Home Guard recruits, who had never previously considered themselves to be military material, were surprised to find themselves become skilled marksmen or good organisers, but even the most well-trained volunteer could do little without access to proper arms and equipment. Doris Ayres' brother was too short at five feet tall to join the forces, but he became an unlikely marksman in the Maidstone GPO Home Guard unit . . .

'He wasn't accepted, of course, for the Army and he couldn't get into the fire service but he was in the Home Guard because he was a postman. He used to have to go to the main post office in Maidstone on duty and go up to the hills to practise firing and come home with his target card which was very interesting because he was really quite good at that. I asked, "What would happen if a paratrooper dropped into the post office?" He said, "I don't really know." I said, "Would you shoot him with your gun?" He replied, "No, because the ammunition is locked up and so and so has the key so I would have to wait for him to come and unlock it."'

It was a source of great relief to many members and their families that the Home Guard was never called upon to use their skills in earnest. There were many times when the alert came and they were always ready to spring into action with whatever resources they had.

Bill Callan testifies:

'One night I remember rather vividly was when we were at the headquarters in Northfleet over near the football ground and suddenly the officer came out and said we'd got a red warning and would we go out on our push bikes and get all the men. It probably was the quickest way because hardly anybody had phones then.

'We charged round and I thought, we're going to do well if the Germans come, we had two rifles and one machine gun. I whipped into my old work place and pinched the bosses double bore shotgun and spent the night in a slit trench halfway up Nash bank waiting for the Germans to come. That was the only time I had been frightened during the war. It suddenly struck me they might come and there was me with a double bore shotgun and four cartridges. That would have fixed the German Army good and proper.'

The Kent Home Guard was far more likely to see real action during the war than its counterparts in less vulnerable counties of England. Colin Cuthbert's Cliftonville Battalion, which provided coastal look-outs in the area, watched the seas for invaders and the skies for attacking aircraft. Colin was on duty one night when a Heinkel bomber crashed in the sea just below their post . . .

'A searchlight came on with a dramatic sort of "click" on the Foreness Point and it swept right around the sea and it gradually came back towards the land where we were. There, illuminated, was the great tall fin of a Heinkel III with the rest of the plane in front of it and a big swastika on the back tail. We thought the war had really started so we ran down to the water's edge and we dug some pretty quick holes and split up; Roy got one side of them and I got the other side, and the idea was that we would catch them in a crossfire if the going got a bit rough. We were full of enthusiasm and we thought we could handle this, Youth! We lay there very very quietly and they got out of the plane and inflated their dinghy all in the glare of the searchlight, it was like a silent film. We only heard the hiss of the dinghy blowing up. There was perfect silence after that. They started paddling very definitely in a marked manner to show they were only paddling and gradually came towards the shore. We didn't say a word, we couldn't do anything except watch them coming towards us. They were within six to eight feet of the water's edge and without saying a word they sat there and put their hands up in the searchlight, very dramatic. They were all done up in their furs and we watched them and of course we had to make a decision, we had to get up and show ourselves. That was not a nice decision to make, but anyway, I got up and went out to the dinghy and said "Put your hands up" and pulled the dinghy into the shore.

'We frisked them for guns or anything we thought they would have, and when they saw that we weren't going to cut up rough with them or shoot them, one of them put his hand inside his jacket and pulled out another revolver which rather shook us because we thought we had all their guns, but we obviously hadn't.'

No shots were fired, and at that moment the Commanding Officer of the Home Guard and the police descended to take the prisoners off to the police station, from where they were eventually sent to Canada. Their plane was the cause of much excitement in the area when daylight came and among the people who turned up to inspect the bomber was Colin's Commanding Officer, who happened to be the local milkman.

'He was also President of the Rifle Club, a red hot man on guns and everybody was there looking at this bomber laying in the bay; he unfortunately pulled the trigger of the machine gun and sprayed the cliffs with bullets, everybody ran for miles and miles and miles.'

Bert Lewis from Sittingbourne belonged to a Home Guard unit which was based at nearby Borden. Their training routines were nothing if not enthusiastic and the unit soon became the scourge of local military establishments.

'We used to go out at night. We had been taken across by the Elmley Ferry through the marshes and into Eastchurch Aerodrome without anybody finding us. People in the Air Force told us off for being there. We also broke through the barriers at Detling and got in there. Our Officer went through and he saw the men on sentry walking up and down so he went up behind and grabbed one and got him down, he wanted to fight. Anyway, they gave us a breakfast, lots of fried corned beef in batter. One man said, "I'm not going to eat that," I'd never had it before but I was hungry so I said I was going to eat it.'

The Borden unit provided more concrete help to the local army by putting a nightly watch on large houses in the area which were used as sleeping quarters for soldiers.

'You had to guard two hours every night and we had a specific place to watch in case anything came along or any planes came down. One did come down at Borden and the Germans in it were all killed. Mainly we looked after the houses where the soldiers were billeted. There were quite a number round Borden way. I suppose it was to let them rest before they went across to France. They did teach us to fire a rifle, that's one thing. We did learn something there.'

During the day Bert worked as a farm labourer from six in the morning until five in the evening. He then went on Home Guard duty, where exercises or guard duties often went on all night and so the county's security rested partly on men who were already worn out from a hard day's work. While in no doubt about the Home Guard's dedication to duty, Bert readily saw the funny side to some of the many scrapes his unit experienced.

'Another time we were out there and they dropped a bomb just off the Staplehurst Road. When the aeroplane blew up and we all dived down a trench, one man there said, "I can't move, I'm stuck." Somebody had gone down there with a fixed bayonet and it had gone through his little gaiter, sticking it to the ground. He couldn't move but it didn't touch his leg at all. Sometimes when it came to ten o'clock, they would say, "Come on" to the Officer, "Time we went for our drink, pubs will be shut," and he used to dismiss them.

'We were going to have a call out one night, they didn't tell us exactly when but we had our full kit ready. I was in lodgings at the time and my landlady said, "The whistle has gone Bert, you had better get ready." So I got ready, all dressed up, put everything on, and set off to parade round a large house. The Officer was there and had seen that everybody was alright. Some man walked along with bedroom slippers on, so the Officer said,

"That's not full kit, why have you got your bedroom slippers on?" He replied, "I thought they wouldn't hear me coming."'

Many Home Guard units were based at or near local pubs, and Bert's battalion was no exception . . .

'Our base was at the May Pole at Borden. We used to do two hours on certain nights and I laid there one night because it wasn't my turn to go out. The Germans dropped a bomb and it went down the well, but it didn't go off. The force of it going down shook our hut which had a tiny little combustion stove. The pipe fell off the stove and across my pillow, I thought it was getting very hot and it was the smoke from the combustion stove, I looked like a black minstrel.'

Although the pub did provide a good meeting place for Home Guard units, it certainly did not help their image as Colin Cuthbert recalls . . .

'Funnily enough most of the platoon commanders were the local publicans. It's not really a thing to boast about nowadays, but in those days it was very convenient because you could go and see the CO there and if it was a cold night, the lads would have a drink and it was very convivial.'

However, Colin also remembers less friendly occasions:

'Sometimes in the dark of winter, down on Pegwell Bay there, when searchlights and blackouts were about it got a bit ghostly and hairy down there, and you felt very much alone.'

After the evacuation of Dunkirk in the early summer of 1940, the German invasion of England seemed inevitable, and the county of Kent would have needed more than the Home Guard to repel the enemy.

Peter Boulden from Aldington recalls the seriousness of the situation:

'They expected at that time and expected is the right word, they expected that the Germans would come, not that they might but that they would come. The higher-ups expected not to be able to hold the coastline, the line of defence was going to be further inland, but they wanted to leave a certain number of people behind who were trained in sabotage to create as much havoc as possible.'

It was the Commander in charge of the forces in the Kent coastal area, General Andrew Thorne, who asked the War Office to provide him with a guerilla force to operate behind enemy lines in the county. He was sent Captain Peter Fleming, the brother of the James Bond author, Ian Fleming. Captain Fleming set up his headquarters at The Garth in Bilting near Ashford, and he had a small group of staff to help him organise the training and facilities needed to create the Auxiliary Units.

One of the people with him was Brigadier Michael Calvert, a member of the Army's Special Operations Executive, who was an expert in demolition work.

'Our job was to raise and train civilians to carry out demolition and I was given a very free hand. We prepared at least four cuts in every road going from the sea to the North Downs. I want to state here the general plan was to hold all the ports in South England and deny the ports to the enemy. The line where they hoped to stop the enemy was along the North Downs and there they built these concrete pill boxes which still exist today and the idea then was that the Germans would be stopped there. Our main reserve and our only armoured division was stationed in the Oxford area so they could go to East Anglia or South East England or South West England wherever action was threatened and counter attack. Our job was to raise a guerilla force between the coast and the North Downs.'

Brigadier Calvert made plans to sabotage each road between the Kent Coast and the North Downs. The plan was that when the Germans had crossed the area, they would find the roads behind them had been destroyed, so effectively cutting their main lines of supply. Calvert decided to recruit four parties of civilians to deal with each main road . . .

'I expected that at least three out of four could think of some jolly good reason why they wouldn't take action. These were farmers whose names were given to us by the Controller or by the General and we trained them and all they had to do really was to put the explosive in place and press a time fuse and then go away.

'We found some of these people were reluctant to do this destruction. They had known Britain for so long so that when we wanted to blow up a bridge they said that bridge was built in 1400 or something. We found this worst in Kent and when Sir Auckland Geddes came and asked me a question regarding the problems I said that the land owners of Kent were very reluctant to help and that they were not co-operating. I remember him saying that the land property owners of Kent were always willing to sacrifice their only sons for their country but not one square yard of their property and I think this dates back centuries. During that time they didn't put Sussex and Kent battalions to defend Kent and Sussex because they realised that they would be reluctant to shell their own towns, so most of the troops were from outside and then we used the Lovat scouts to act as pump primers. There were three civilian parties besides the demolition party and most civilians would not normally shoot Germans and German sentries and German officers.

'It was difficult to get the odd farmer to shoot a General. You can imagine that the Germans would probably behave very politely and pay for every-thing and so we wanted to start the ball rolling. Therefore we recruited Lovat Scouts and their job was to shoot Germans in the back and then the Germans would have retribution and shoot Kentish Men and Men of Kent and Sussex in the back and this would rouse the anger of the local population who would then start shooting Germans. It struck me as an interesting development of war.'

This innocuous-looking diary and calendar were issued to men in the Auxiliary Units. They were actually handbooks of instructions in lethal sabotage. (D. Pugh)

The Lovat Scouts were an elite band of soldiers which later became the Commandos, and fortunately they never had to carry out the brutal task that Brigadier Calvert describes. One platoon was based with Peter Fleming in Bilting and helped in the training of new recruits to the Auxiliary Units. Biddy Allen lived nearby, and recalls seeing the Lovat Scouts, although at the time she didn't know who they were or what they were doing . . . in wartime it was safer not to know . . .

'Lord Lovat came and set up this team of men here who were really working at night keeping in touch with those other points like Charing at the top of the hill there and another one down over towards Bridge. You wouldn't see them in the day but at night-time you would hear the sounds and see lights and then they developed into the first Commandos and they were the guardians against the first invasion. They would have been in the first line of men. These were the men who usually helped me to turn the mushroom compost when they were off duty.'

Peter Fleming was responsible for master-minding the recruitment and training of the Auxiliary Units until he was replaced in November 1940 by Lieutenant

Colonel Norman Field. Each unit consisted of a patrol of six men and a leader, and the recruits were all hand-picked for their local knowledge. Farmers were a popular choice, for their good knowledge of the country areas, and experience of firearms. Tom Miller had a fruit farm at Eastry near Sandwich, and the first he heard about the Auxiliary Units was when his friend Guy Steed and a uniformed officer called at his farmhouse and asked him if he would be interested in tackling the Germans if they came . . .

'Because I was a little bit that way inclined anyhow just before the war I'd cut down some trees and used some gelignite to get the roots out of the ground but I hadn't quite used it all. I suppose I shouldn't have kept it but I did, and I was telling this Lieutenant that I had this explosive and that if the worst came to the worst and I got the chance I would be happy to try and blow up a German armoured car or something with it, if it came near me. He said, "We're looking for your sort of chap, if you would like to sign this paper, I'll tell you more about it." He pulled the paper out of his pocket and it was the Official Secrets Act, and when I signed it on the back I saw the names of people that I knew who had already joined. So I said yes, rather! I'll carry on there and that is how it started.'

Guy Steed turned out to be the leader of the Sandwich group, and his brother Norman belonged to the Thanet Auxiliary Unit. As with many of the new recruits to the Auxiliary Units, Norman was already a member of the Home Guard when he was approached to join . . .

'Billy Gardner of Birchington came to see me on the farm and he brought an officer in uniform and put the whole thing to me. Was I prepared to join an organisation of saboteurs? Of course it was couched in different language from just that and I was led up the garden path for quite a long time before it was divulged what was intended. It was quite clearly laid on the line for me to understand that it was a secret organisation in the event of an invasion and that I would be trained to perform certain duties in the Home Guard of which I was a member and I would be part of a separate unit. I think it was Captain Field who came at that time, not Fleming, but Fleming I met later.'

The new recruits did not know what they were letting themselves in for until they had signed the Official Secrets Act, but contrary to Brigadier Calvert's fears that Kent's farmers would be reluctant to take part in acts of sabotage, most of the Auxiliaries were keen to do something to help their country. Percy Clarke became a member of one of the vital Romney Marsh patrols, and recalls that he was at work on the day that a group of unexpected visitors called to see him . . .

'Captain Field, Peter Fleming and there was a third one who when I was introduced to him it didn't register but he had red tags on his collar so I knew he was very high up and sometime afterwards I was told it was Montgomery who was in the area at the time. I was then asked whether I would form a seven-man patrol, this was on a Friday afternoon, and they gave me until Saturday evening to find seven men, to take up to The Garth, the Headquarters, and they would arrange transport for us to start training on the Sunday.'

There were four Auxiliary Unit patrols on Romney Marsh, called Mushroom, Truffle, Toadstool and Fungus. They would have been the first in line to face the German invaders, but if the Germans had come, each patrol had to operate independently. They had no contact with the other patrols and in most cases did not even know where they were based. Like Percy Clarke, Dick Body from Snargate became the leader of one of these patrols. In Dick's case, it was a Captain Allnatt who approached him with the idea . . .

'He came along and asked whether I was in the Home Guard. I said I was. He said, "That doesn't matter, can you find six others to come in and join an organisation? The main thing is that they must have good local knowledge, if you can't find six I know of two chaps who will come with you."'

Having signed the Official Secrets Act, the new recruits to the Auxiliary Units learned how they would be expected to fight the German invaders in Kent. Tom Miller explains:

'We were to conduct acts of sabotage against any German troops or vehicles that landed and particularly their supplies, their ammunition dumps if they had left any ammunition about and their petrol supplies. That was the leading role because if they came over here they would need vehicles and they would find no fuel here as all the petrol pumps were empty. There was no petrol to be had at any of the village garages and there was only one petrol pump in the area and that was in Sandwich. If we wanted petrol we all had to go to that one petrol pump and that was the only one. Presumably if the Germans had landed, arrangements were made to blow that up or set it on fire. They made quite sure that the Germans wouldn't find any petrol in the area or any fuel of any sort.'

Sabotaging German fuel supplies was only one aspect of the work the auxiliaries were expected to do. As Dick Body recalls, they would also have had to try and destroy the Germans' means of transport and their weapons.

'Our first targets were to be lorries, dumps, fuel tanks and stores. Later the emphasis was on interfering with communications.'

There were approximately thirty separate Auxiliary Units in Kent, each made up of a patrol of seven. They all received Home Guard uniforms, since membership of the Home Guard could act as a cover to quell any local suspicion about the nature of their activities. Their names, however, did not appear on any official register, which made them technically outside the rules of the Geneva Convention, so the Germans could have shot them on capture. The units operated from twenty-eight specially constructed hide-outs that were cleverly concealed and dotted all over the county. They were called operational bases or OBs, and were usually constructed by engineers from outside Kent. Peter Boulden explains:

'Dug outs where we kept the ammunition and explosives were totally secret. A unit of the Army dug all of these and were brought down from the North Country. They were taken back again so that even the local Army did not know where they were so they couldn't have given them away.'

George Freeland was in the Fungus patrol of the Romney Marsh area and was already in the Home Guard when he was asked to join the Auxiliary Units. As with all the OBs, the exact location of their base was a well-kept secret, hidden among the trees in Rolvenden woods.

'There was a hole in the ground covered with a mat and steps going vertically down into a cave. It was built by the Royal Engineers and there were bunks for sleeping in, food and a loo and as soon as the enemy arrived we were supposed to disappear at night and go in there.'

Tom Miller's patrol near Sandwich had a secondary hide, big enough to hold one man, situated beside the main Dover Road so that they could observe enemy troop movements. The group's main OB was hidden in Betteshanger woods . . .

'It was built by the engineers and it was an underground chamber dug almost into the side of a chalk pit but the face of the chalk was rather cleverly hidden. When they dug the chalk out they saved it somehow and made it look as if it was just a pile of chalk against the side. There was no indication that there was any kind of room inside. At the far end of the room you could go up the short ladder or stairway and there was a lid at the top, open the lid and you were in Betteshanger woods.'

The entrances to the OBs were always cleverly hidden, concealed by earth and leaves or even under the roots of an old tree stump. The hides contained enough food and supplies to sustain the patrol for at least a fortnight. One of the most spectacular hide-outs was a huge underground chamber built at Godmersham Park near Ashford. It was big enough to house, sleep and feed 120 people, and was built to provide an emergency sanctuary for auxiliaries on the run from Germans. The underground hides on Romney Marsh were below sea level, so had to be watertight to prevent them flooding. The hide used by Dick Body's patrol was built by a Maidstone firm, and cost about £300. He describes the facilities:

'Our base was actually in a sheep pound fairly central for all the patrol. Solidly constructed, concrete, lime wood bitumen and then white tiles inside. In each OB, as we called them, were bunks for six, very well constructed, but the boards were hard and we very soon removed the boards and put up wire netting. A patrol being seven, six were able to sleep and the seventh was on the alert. There was a substantial table and benches each side which formed cupboards for storing things. There was also a fifty gallon galvanised water tank and an Elsan closet.'

The main OB used by Norman Steed's Thanet unit was built by the Army, making use of an old chalk pit.

'It had a vertical shaft created and an entrance and exit at the base. It was a room into which six beds had to be placed in two tiers and we had to have all the other facilities such as a toilet, food store and ammunition and weapon store, but it was quite small, roughly about twelve to fourteen feet by eight feet. We had a secret method of getting into it as it was well hidden. Subsequently, we decided that we wanted a base elsewhere and we ourselves created one at Nash Court in an old cellar of the original farmhouse that had been burned down. Adjoining that was an old underground chapel and we created in this area our own operational base.'

Since their work was so specialised, the Auxiliary Units had to be highly trained. Much of the training was carried out at the Kent Headquarters at The Garth in Bilting, and the various patrols were brought in for weekends of intensive training. Percy Clarke recalls some of those early lectures.

'First thing they gave us a basic idea of explosive booby traps and everything we were expected to handle and we were soon kitted out with what little gear they had at the time. The lectures were very very interesting indeed, lectures on explosives and then demonstrations and you could try yourself. We soon got quite professional, or we thought we did.'

The training sessions and exercises at The Garth were the only opportunity the auxiliaries had to meet members of other patrols, but for safety they were not allowed to know who they were, or where their bases were situated. Besides, their thoughts were full of the task in hand, learning to sabotage the supplies and equipment of the German invaders as Norman Steed remembers:

'We had to place explosives on any of the German equipment, be it aircraft, tanks or what have you and we were trained in the use of sticky bombs, explosives with time switches so that we could place them in position and get away to safety. We were shown methods of approach and trained in night travel and one could get into all sorts of difficult places to place the explosives. We were, unfortunately, issued with some very strong wire that we would be told to stretch across the road when the motor-cyclists were coming. A terrible thing to do but we never did use them.

'We had training subsequently, once we were told what to do and how to do it, with the Army. The Army were prepared to play with us as it were in a game of war and our job was to try and show that we had spotted them and blown them up.'

Even though the Army helped in the training of the Auxiliary Units, it did not know the exact nature of their work, and assumed it was just the Home Guard on manoeuvres. Although the Auxiliary Units were started up in Kent and Sussex, the organisation eventually spread all over the country. The national headquarters was at Coleshill in Wiltshire, and most of the auxiliaries went there for special training weekends. There they practised attacking imaginary targets and had more lectures on all aspects of guerilla warfare as Peter Boulden recalls:

'We were trained in all aspects of warfare, trained very thoroughly by what subsequently turned out to be the Commando Units. We were trained to kill with our hands, we were trained in unarmed combat, we were trained in all weapons from machine gun down to pistols. We had pistols issued. We were given knives and taught how to kill with them. We were taught to use all forms of explosives with three or four different varieties of fuse, some of which were instantaneous and some were long and others longer, depending on what we wanted to do. We were taught to set booby traps.

'The main part of the training was really to teach us what targets to look out for, how to get ourselves away from the target area and to take care of ourselves as long as possible. I think the powers that be rather thought that our life span might not be too long.'

Norman Steed was among those who travelled to Wiltshire for training, along with the rest of the Thanet patrol. Although the training they received was far more specialised and more thorough than that received by soldiers in the regular Army, the auxiliaries were still technically civilians, so some of the finer points of military etiquette were a mystery to them, as Norman explains:

'We would travel right through London without a tie on and in those days they thought we were undressed, but we didn't bother, we hadn't had any instructions. One other instruction we had never had was how to salute. If a superior officer walked by and we were looking in a shop window, we carried on looking in a shop window, because we didn't know how to salute, at least I did because I had done it but other than my young brother, none of the others had any idea how to salute an officer or who to salute. And the outcome of that was there was a directive which came through from Headquarters somewhere to our unit and we were then put through the instructions of what to wear. We had to always wear a tie when we were travelling and shown how to salute. There we were, we were a pretty rabbley rough lot.'

The Auxiliary Units were well-armed and equipped, usually more so than the Home Guard and sometimes more so than their counterparts in the Army. As Tom Miller recalls, this may have had something to do with the fact that the auxiliaries had friends in high places . . .

'The thing we were most proud of was that we were given revolvers. That was quite something because the Army people we trained with were very jealous because we didn't tell them what we were doing, so when they found we had revolvers they said, "The bloody Home Guard are getting revolvers, we don't have them." I understand it was because of Winston Churchill. Nobody was told very much about what we were doing, but of course Winston Churchill being the Prime Minister had to be told what was happening and on the report of what we were doing, so I'm told, he just scribbled in the margin, "Give these men revolvers", and that's all there was to it.'

The revolvers were just part of the armoury that was available to the Auxiliary Units, but a variety of weapons was necessary to enable the auxiliaries to carry out their work. Norman Steed remembers:

'We were issued with first class weapons which came from America, 38 pistol, a 22 peep sized rifle and several other small arms that we were allowed to use. We didn't have any noisy weapons, the 22 was supposed to be able to pick off individual persons and of course we were issued with explosives and fuse wires, trip wires and all the paraphernalia we required.'

A special sticky bomb was devised to place on German tanks and military vehicles. As Tom Miller explains, although the sticky bombs looked good on paper, in practice they were next to useless.

'We tried these things up at The Garth, trying to throw them at vehicles and various things and we found they were no use. From a practical point of view anything that had been along a country road was covered in dust and of course the sticky bomb would not stick to dust, it just stuck there for a second or two and flopped off, so we abandoned that idea. Still it was a good job to have tried it out.'

Although the Auxiliary Units were issued with firearms, it was not intended that they should become involved in a battle with the Germans — their job was strictly sabotage, although as Tom Miller explains, this could mean killing some- one to accomplish the task:

'Shooting wasn't really our job. In fact we were told not to get involved in a fight with the Germans, because we almost certainly would have come off worst if we did. We were to keep out of their way. Our job was in sabotage and setting fire to their petrol pumps and blowing up their explosive dumps and disabling their vehicles. Killing Germans was quite secondary, we were only to kill the Germans if we had to. If there was a guard, we might have to quietly go and kill him first before we could get to the target. I don't know how I should have managed it but we were given daggers and told how to kill a man silently. Mentality in the war was a little bit different. If you think about it in these times you think how horrible but in war you have to think, "It's either him or me."'

Dick Body recalls that while at the Auxiliary Units' Wiltshire headquarters, they received some rather sinister training in unarmed combat from Army PT instructors . . .

'I particularly remember what could be done with the rim of a steel helmet and also the sharp heel of a boot.'

All members of the Auxiliary Units recognised that secrecy was of paramount importance. It was vital that no one discovered the whereabouts of their OBs or hides, or the security of a whole unit could be jeopardised. Even the auxiliaries' wives and families were not told about their work.

The Home Guard provided a good cover for the auxiliaries who could use it to explain away their long absences from home and their dishevelled state after coming back from training exercises. The secrecy was also to protect the auxiliaries' wives and families, as Tom Miller explains:

'Our alibi was that we were scouting and signalling. That was our job. We were a branch of the Home Guard and we didn't need any more than that. They didn't know where we were. The great thing was for nobody else to know as Captain Field pointed out, other people should not know what we were doing, it was their chief safety and our chief safety. If we were captured, skilled interrogators would soon find out if you really didn't know or if you were withholding information.'

Although the auxiliaries knew that there were other patrols in existence, and even met members of them at training weekends, it was again vital that they did not know where they were based, so that if one auxiliary was captured, he could not sacrifice the whole operation and the three thousand or so men that were involved in it, but secrecy had its price, as Norman Steed recalls . . .

'We were instructed that if any of our six unit were injured and couldn't be saved we would have to shoot him or kill him some way or the other. We were instructed how best to do this. A terrible thing to have to do but it was our instruction. In other words, not one of our six unit could be captured alive otherwise he could be forced to divulge the rest of it. Very worrying indeed because they were all my friends, one of whom was my brother. I was only so grateful it never had to happen.'

There was also the hint that any passer-by who had accidentally stumbled on an OB would have had to be killed to protect the units in the event of an invasion. Although the majority of the auxiliaries in Kent were able to keep their work secret, there were those who were not so discreet and could not resist letting out some snippets of information about their secret assignation, as Tom Miller remembers:

'There was one member of the Canterbury group who talked about the sort of thing that he was doing and he said, "I mustn't tell you too much about it." He told people his secret a little bit of this and a little bit of that till at last someone, not a member of the group at all, came to him and gave him a complete description of what he was doing. There was no secrecy at all so what did they do, they had to take the other man into the group.'

The main purpose of the Auxiliary Units had always been to remain behind enemy lines if the Germans came, so that their local knowledge could be used to best advantage. But as D Day approached in 1944, there were suggestions that the auxiliaries could have been sent to France to help out if the Normandy landings went wrong. George Freeland recalls being asked.

'We were called to a very secret meeting in the Marshes and we were addressed by a high ranking officer who told us that there was going to be an invasion, a D Day, and if things went wrong and there were defeats or delays, we were asked to parachute behind the lines and join the Free French as saboteurs.'

So how did George, a civilian trained in demolition and sabotage, feel about being asked to leave his family behind and fight on unknown territory?

'Shocking! I asked, "What about our wives and families? What provision is made for them?" He said, "Nothing." I don't think I would have volunteered but fortunately we were victorious, we were never asked to do so.'

During the war the Auxiliary Units never knew when they might be called upon to leave their families behind and begin living and operating as saboteurs in the teeth of the German Army. For most of them, as Norman Steed describes, it was a time of great personal stress . . .

'It was always there. I wondered what was going to happen to my wife, and by that time we had two children and it was worrying but it was our effort towards the war in a very minor degree in respect of those that went into the Army and were killed outright.'

The auxiliaries were fully armed, trained and ready to go into action at a moment's notice. Peter Boulden answers an obvious question:

'One of the questions we have been asked many times since, especially now, forty to fifty years later is, "Would you really have killed Germans?" And the answer to that is quite easy, of course we would have done. Our parents were in the First World War, we were brought up in the shadow of that and there weren't exactly good feelings towards Germans. But that wasn't the point, the point was we were not going to allow Germans to run around our country.'

Fifty years later the surviving members of Kent's Secret Army, the Auxiliary Units, can look back at their wartime adventures and talk about them openly with a sense of relief that they were never called upon to go into action.

Percy Clarke has the final word:

'It was very exciting at the time but as I said, we were pleased it did not happen, but we would have been ready. We would have caused some havoc somehow.'

Chapter VII
THE DUNKIRK SPIRIT

The summer of 1940 was one of the most crucial periods of the Second World War for the Allies and the people of Kent as they gained first-hand experience of the horrors of war, especially when a large percentage of the troops evacuated from Dunkirk and the surrounding beaches in May and June of that year were brought through the ports of Dover, Folkestone, Margate and Ramsgate. The so-called 'phoney war' had come to an end on 9th April 1940 when Hitler invaded Denmark and Norway.

By May the Germans were able to launch their attack on Belgium and Holland, but for the ordinary British soldier the first taste of war came in France and Belgium in a devastating blitzkrieg offensive. The German Army swept through the country bombing everything and anything in its path. The only means of escape was to head for the coast and soldiers and civilians alike made for the Channel ports. The attack caught the allied forces off guard because many soldiers up until then had seen little fighting at all. This was to be their first experience of war. Some soldiers were still in their teens and they found themselves to be ill-equipped and badly prepared.

Leslie Page from Chatham was a soldier with the 44th Division of the Royal Army Ordinance Corps. His introduction to the war was totally relaxed. Billeted in Belgium, his time was spent in cafés enjoying a coffee and a chat. To bridge the inevitable language barrier, Leslie had been issued with a phrase book called 'Flirt' to enable him to enjoy the company of French-speaking young ladies.

Prior to his posting Leslie had been drilling with a broom handle. He was just twenty years old at the time of Dunkirk. 'The training was nowhere near good enough for what we were going to be up against when the time came. We really hadn't had any drills and of course the enemy was equipped with machine pistols and automatic weapons and our Lee Enfield rifles were only single shot, so you had to be very careful of what you got into.'

The situation for allied troops in France had been getting progressively worse. The British, French and Belgium armies had been pushed back to the coast by a well-equipped and rapidly advancing German Army. At home fears were rising that the British troops, the 10th Division of the British Expeditionary Force under the command of General Gort, would become trapped and taken prisoner, thereby removing a large percentage of our fighting force. The evacuation of the troops was becoming inevitable and, as the only avenue of escape was by sea, time was of the essence.

Leslie Page prior to embarkation to France
in 1940.   (L. Page)

By 26th May the German Army had successfully taken Boulogne, isolated Calais and was raining bombs on Dunkirk.

At 10.30 am that morning the Secretary of State for War, Anthony Eden, sent a telegram to General Gort warning him about the possibility of evacuation. Assurances were given that the Navy would provide a fleet of ships and small boats and the RAF would provide support in the air; what the telegram did not say was that Kent, just twenty-one miles from the French coast, was to be in the forefront of this operation.

The evacuation of the allied troops from Dunkirk between 26th May and 4th June 1940 was known as 'Operation Dynamo'. Admiral Sir Bertram Ramsay undertook responsibility for the operation from a gallery in the East Cliff below Dover Castle which local rumour maintained was safe from enemy attack as Eileen Dykes, who lived in the town, recalls:

'There was a rumour around here during the war, I don't know how true it was, that Hitler didn't want to bomb Dover Castle because he reckoned when he came to England he was going to have his first meal there.'

Admiral Ramsay ordered the first ships to France as early as 3.00 pm on the afternoon of the 26th, although the official signal to evacuate was not given by the Admiralty until three minutes to seven, nearly four hours later. By 10.30 pm the first shipment of troops disembarked at Dover and by midnight almost 28,000 men had returned to England. The evacuation of Dunkirk was underway.

Nineteen-year-old George Sone from Gillingham, a despatch rider with the Royal Corps of Signals, was ordered to take the message to the French Commander. Tired from several days marching, he did not realise the significance of the piece of paper he was ordered to carry. 'An RA Officer came along and said, "I want you to do a delivery of a message." I said, "I'm not moving, my Officer told me we'd got to have a rest."'

'He gave me orders that I'd got to do this journey, I was the one to do it. I still refused so he went and got my Officer and he said, "I'm sorry son, but you've got to do this one, this is special." I could have been shot for disobeying an order. I took this order travelling on my motorbike and I dropped off to sleep. I didn't realise it but I hit a French car head-on and landed in a ditch. Two French Officers pulled me out, they questioned me as to where I was going and I questioned them as to who they were. They were in fact the people I had been sent to contact, so I handed over my despatch and this despatch, I found out during the course of conversation, was that we were evacuating. The despatch was the order for the French to withdraw as well.'

The soldiers were told to make for Dunkirk, the only port still in allied hands, although the Luftwaffe had successfully bombed the oil tanks surrounding the port and the raging fires provided a constant landmark for the retreating soldiers, as Leslie Page remembers:

'Shelling started and our vehicles were parked all around. We got into them and drove along the road heading away from the shelling. I remember our Colonel standing on the crossroads and he waved us all up the road away from the crossroads because the Jerry tanks were coming, so we got out of there very quickly. I remember jumping into a hedge of stinging nettles with the shells dropping around us and we were suddenly awakened to the fact that this was war.

'As we drove through the towns, which were being bombed by Jerry planes, the Luftwaffe was doing a great job and we realised we could not hit back at planes with the weapons we had, so we were just going to be running away from the destruction.'

'The roads were full of refugees and we came to understand that this was a general retreat, there were nuns, fifth columnists, you didn't know who the people were. Carriages being pulled by horses who broke free when the planes were shelling and then the Luftwaffe started strafing the roads so we all scattered across the fields and I remember the lorries were loaded with civilians. I asked someone where we were going and he said, "Well you see that smoke in the sky, that's Dunkirk, make for that," which we did.'

John Curley, a twenty-year-old from Dover, was in the Royal Army Service Corps, part of the 50th Division. He was in a tiny village just outside Arras when the order came through.

'We got battered, we got shelled and bombed and finally we got the order to evacuate. Somebody said, I think it was our Commanding Officer, "The place I think we have to make for is Dunkirk so if you get isolated, remember the name Dunkirk." Well I'll never forget it.'

Stanley Caleno from Meopham, serving with his regiment the Royal Army Service Corps, recalls his orders:

'Just before we pulled out the Major sent for me and asked me to collect all the silver from the Officers' Mess and take it to a wood and bury it, which I did. I thought the situation must be getting nasty.'

John Plested from Folkestone was another involved with precious metal when instructions came:

'We were in Brussels unloading gold bullion out of a bank which we took to Ostend. It was sent to England by destroyer. As we cleared the bank Jerry was coming in at the other end of the city.'

The long straight roads of France were clogged with refugees, pushing hand carts laden with their worldly possessions and as a result the journey to Dunkirk for the soldiers was laboriously slow, often hampered by German gunfire as John Curley recalls:

'We were told to take our trucks as far as we could to the coast and then abandon them, but we couldn't move, the refugees were streaming onto the roads. The Germans, with their blitzkreig tactics, we never realised how brutal they could be, because they were just coming down flying along these roads which in France are dead straight, and there were thousands of refugees. The Germans were just blazing away with their machine guns and we couldn't move, we couldn't get through.'

Mary Sullivan from Hythe had joined the Council of Voluntary War Workers as a joke and was sent to man a canteen in France.

'We saw more bombing raids than we wanted. The military came in the canteen one day and said, "Be out in four minutes." Luckily we had a mobile canteen.'

Mary was twenty-six years old and was reported missing but eventually reached the Dunkirk beach where she and fellow Salvation Army volunteers tried to keep up troop morale. Naval staff at Dover ensured that all ships, however small, could get stores, fuel, provisions and charts, but despite all the information that was provided beforehand, it was not until the second day of the operation that the difficulties facing the rescuers became apparent.

For centuries the stretch of coastline encompassing the port of Dunkirk had been known for its treachery. The whole area was subject to strong tidal currents and there were no beacons to guide the ships. It was impossible to use the main harbour at Dunkirk because it had been blocked by an air attack seven days earlier. The only two points left were a jetty to the west of the harbour and the East Mole, a wooden structure thrusting out into the sea from the Channel, but within days this too had been bombed. The Navy was forced to construct a little platform of planks from which the soldiers could jump onto the boats, but the greatest danger facing rescuers and troops alike was the constant shelling which battered the area for the full ten days of the operation.

William Hewitt from Broadstairs was a Sub-Lieutenant aboard the mine sweeper, HMS *Sutton*. He had experienced bombing before but the dive-bombing attacks of the Luftwaffe at this time truly frightened him.

'In the first two days we had several dive-bombing attacks and they were a very different matter. There was no way they could miss. They were Stukas and they would come over at a fairly modest height, around 2,000 feet, until they picked out the particular ship they wanted to attack and then they would come down vertically, straight down on top of the ship. You could see the bomb leave the aircraft as it pulled out of the dive and lifted away. The bomb would come straight for you, that was very unnerving, especially as the Germans had fitted sirens and they made a terrible screeching noise. You felt this bomb was for you personally and they were very big bombs indeed.'

The troops still making their way to Dunkirk were tired and hungry. John Curley remembers being ordered to live off the land, 'But we weren't allowed to loot. Anyone caught looting would be shot, but we could take what food was necessary from farms.'

Unlike many, Ron Mercer from Saltwood, in the Fourth Battalion of Buffs, was fortunate, 'We scrounged plenty of food, there was plenty of food about in the farmhouses. We were killing the chicken and pigs and had soup, there was plenty of vegetables at that time of the year, and stews. But obviously we were tired, we had marched twenty miles or so and wouldn't remember it, we were actually asleep on a march.'

Harry Pickett whose parents were living in West Farleigh, near Maidstone, was another lucky soldier. There were ex-butchers in his regiment and shortly before marching down into Dunkirk one of them killed a lamb and skinned it and the soldiers sat in a ditch by the canal eating roast lamb and passing it up and down the line from one to another.

Eric Pemberton, who was evacuated from the Dunkirk beaches by the Ramsgate Life Boat crew, recalls having been without food or drink for four days, his last meal being the curious combination of rum and beetroot as there was no other food available.

The Dunkirk water supply had been cut off by the bombing and there was a serious shortage of water, although not necessarily of other things to drink. Leslie Page recalls his walk into the town:

'There was a despatch rider lying in the road beside his bike and I thought that's a dead despatch rider — this is what it's all about, you were coming across bodies. Then in the cellars of the houses in the town were soldiers trying to find something to eat and drink, which was mostly bottles of wine. I walked across the bridge and as I walked some chap came across with bottles of champagne in his arms, and handed me one. I walked onto the beach and it was just like going to any seaside town, until you got on the beach and there were all shell holes, troops and lorries all driven down onto the sand. I just jumped into a shell hole and opened this bottle of champagne and drank it. Jerry was strafing, machine gunning all the beaches up and down, it was just like a dream, you couldn't believe it. I was so young and inexperienced, to go to war like that was quite a shock.'

The weather on the third day of evacuation was bad for flying, misty and overcast and as a result the flow of men who made it safely back to England increased quite markedly.

Seventeen vessels arrived at Dover at once in the early hours of that May morning including 15,000 French troops. The port was temporarily closed while the backlog was dealt with and many ships were re-routed to Newhaven and Southampton.

William Hewitt recalls being sent to La Panne where it was the Captain's job to see if it was possible to rescue any men from that beach. When they arrived they found the beach was ideal. He was up on the bridge with the Captain and takes up the tale:

'After waiting for an hour with no signal from the beach, we tried a shaded light and nothing happened. The Captain sat in his chair behind the bridge and finally said we should send a boat ashore. It was pretty obvious the First Lieutenant and the Navigator didn't fancy it, the Navigator disappeared into the chart house and the First Lieutenant went down the ladder — we didn't see them again. I was a bit tired of sitting around on the bridge with nothing happening and so I volunteered. The Captain said I'd better go down below and get kitted out.

'I think he couldn't risk his Navigator or any of his Officers ashore and I was the Sub-Lieutenant and I was a reservist as well, after all he didn't know whether there were any Germans on the beach or not and I think he felt I was the best chap to go.

'I had told the Coxswain of the whaler, a leading seaman, to lay of fifty yards from the beach so that he could get back to the ship if he needed to. I went over the side of the whaler and waded ashore, I couldn't see very far but the beach was absolutely deserted and absolutely quiet except for this rumbling gun-fire in the background. I seemed to be totally alone but I had the feeling there were a lot of people looking at me. It was pitch dark and I thought I'd walk inshore. I walked across the beach, there was dead low water and as I walked across into the range of these big sand hills, three figures rose up and walked towards me. I stopped and I thought they might be Germans in plain clothes. I pulled out the revolver and I suddenly remembered I'd forgotten to put bullets in it. I waved it at them and they disappeared. I walked through these sand hills up the coastal road then turned left away from Dunkirk, which was burning. Ahead of me I heard marching feet and I knew they were soldiers so I jumped into a ditch, I didn't know it was full of barbed wire.

'Anyway, I extricated myself from this by the time the soldiers had marched past and I suddenly heard English voices, well they were cursing and swearing, so I knew they were English. I ran after them, a Sergeant and two soldiers, I was soaking wet and dishevelled-looking and I'd lost my cap — after all I had been in five feet of water. I caught them up and explained we had a ship waiting, but it must have seemed a pretty implausible story to them. Fortunately they eventually believed it in rather a grudging fashion. On the way down I hoped to God the whaler was still there, or they would have thought I was having them on. They were Royal Engineers, the first soldiers taken off the beach there and by dawn we had taken off two hundred men with their rifles and equipment.'

For those waiting on the beaches in the North of France, 28th May saw the arrival of the first of the 'little ships'; 655 small craft went across to France, many from the Thames Estuary and the Kent ports. An appeal had been read out to the nation after the nine o'clock news on 14th May: 'All owners of self-propelled pleasure craft between thirty and one hundred feet in length are requested to send the particulars of these vessels to the Admiralty within fourteen days'.

This met with an immediate and enthusiastic response.

Staff who lived on the premises of the Bon Marche departmental store in Gravesend had a special preview, as Joan Chinery explains:

'In the evenings we used to go on to the flat roof which had a marvellous view of the Thames and Tilbury Docks. We were sitting up there in deck-chairs on this beautiful summer evening when all of a sudden we noticed ships all moving down to the Thames estuary. We couldn't make out what was happening. We sat up there for a couple of hours and still they were coming — some up from Tilbury Docks. Tugs pulling rowing boats, every-thing on the move. Next morning I went up and there wasn't a ship any-where on the river or in the docks.'

Barges, dredgers, trawlers, shrimping and cockle boats, paddle steamers such as the *Medway Queen*, even a mud hopper, eventually made the trip to France, manned by crews of willing volunteers. Many of those who came forward were still in their teens and played a vital role in providing a ferry service from the

FLIRT

I feel I am going to love you passionately.
Je sens que je vais vous aimer passionnément.
zhe' sau** ke' zhe' vay voo zay-may pass-ce-oh-nay-mau**

I should like to kiss you again.
Je voudrais vous embrasser encore.
zhe' voo-dray voo zau**-brah-say au**-kohr

You do make me so unhappy.
Vous me rendez très malheureux.
voo me' rau**-day tray mahl-e'-re'

I should like a photo of you.
Je voudrais une photo de vous.
zhe voo-dray zün' foh-toh de' voo

I promise you to be good.
Je vous promets d'être sage.
zhe' voo prob-may dett-re' sahzh

I shall never forget you.
Je ne vous oublierai jamais.
zhe' ne' voo zoo-blee-ray zhah.may

I could not do without you.
Je ne saurais plus me passer de vous.
zhe' ne' soh-ray plü me' pah-say de' voo

You are not crossed ?
Vous n'êtes pas fâchée ?
voo nett pah fah-shay

Please, stay still with me a little white.
Restez encore un moment avec moi.
ray-tay zau**-kohr u** moh-mau** ah-veck mwah

Promise you will come again.
Promettez-moi de revenir.
prob-may-tay mwah de' re'-ve'-neer

FLIRT

— 29 —

Si mes parents me voyaient !
Fancy, my parents should see me !
fron'-sé mat pè-rents chould sî mî

Je vais réfléchir.
I shall think it over.
aî chall sinnk it ô'-veur

Serrez-moi bien fort dans vos bras.
Hold me close in your arms.
hold mi clox inn your ârms

Attention, on nous regarde.
Mind. Somebody is looking at us.
maïnnd som-bo'-dé iz loukinn' at euss

Vous êtes trop pressé. Ayez de la patience.
You are in such a hurry. Do take patience.
you âr inn seutch è heur'-ré dou tè'k pé'-chiuns

Je n'aime que vous.
You are the only one I love.
you âr ði ônn'-lé ouann aï lov

Je n'oublierai jamais les heures passées avec vous.
I shall never forget the time I spent with you.
aî chall né'-veur for-guett œ taïm aï spennt ouiz you

Soyez sage.
Be good.
bî goudd

Dire qu'il faut déjà nous quitter.
It is a pity we must part so soon.
it iz è pi'-té ouî meust parti sô sôunn

Qu'allez-vous penser de moi.
What will you think of me.
houott ouil you sinnk of mî

War Department issue shaving brush and razor together with a booklet of French Conversation, entitled FLIRT! Essential equipment for men joining the British Expeditionary Force. The FLIRT booklet was printed in Lille and as far as Leslie Page was concerned eased the plight of the British soldier. His copy is inscribed with the message (in French) 'With the hope that you will soon come back to see us. Good Luck, Cecile.'   (L. Page)

beaches to the larger vessels moored in deeper water further off-shore. For the civilian crews, it was a terrifying experience. The boats were often capsized by the number of desperate and frightened men trying to clamber aboard. The little ships were frequently bombed or torpedoed, discharging their cargo of men into a oil-filled sea.

Eddie Fryer from Gravesend was a fifteen-year-old boy cook on the tug *Tango*:

'Our Captain known as Tango Harry was ordered to round up all barges and small craft and herd them into Tilbury. Later we were told to proceed to Ramsgate with the small craft. We had about twenty of them in tow and we loaded supplies from Ramsgate and went on to Dunkirk. The sea was flat calm and everywhere you could see these small craft rowing into the beaches which were covered with troops. Some of the sailing barges took ammunition across to the beaches for the supplies to help fight off the Germans.

'I remained on board to do as much cooking as possible, soup and mash, corned beef hash, to feed anybody who came aboard, large pots of tea and cocoa. The troops were really tired and bedraggled. We took two or three hundred back to Ramsgate, collected more supplies and went straight back to Dunkirk. We did this trip three times and then on the last occasion, we went into the harbour alongside the *Mole* and took on board 50% British and 50% French troops who had been fighting the rear guard. As we left we could actually see the Germans approaching Dunkirk with lots of artillery fire, just one huge cloud of smoke and mist all along the horizon.'

The sight of the British soldiers, their uniforms in tatters, many covered in oil or naked except for a blanket, brought home the reality of war to the people of Kent.

Mary Cannon worked at the Pavilion Café at the entrance to the East Pier in Ramsgate.

'Being just nineteen I didn't realise the significance of what was going on, I'd never heard of Dunkirk before, didn't even know where Dunkirk was until our local boatman came in and said, "Did you know that Dunkirk is on fire and all our soldiers are on the beaches being bombed and machine gunned?" I said to him innocently enough, "Where is Dunkirk?"

'I didn't have a clue. Then we could see all the small boats coming into the pier head and all the people coming off. Some of them were crawling, some just walking slowly and the terror on their faces was absolutely . . . well you can't describe it. Their uniforms were torn, they were filthy, they smelt. You could smell them, you could literally smell them.'

Alison Ashford, as a schoolgirl, was helping on Folkestone central station and recalls: 'Their eyes had stunned fear in them. Some men were bitter. They felt their mates had deserted them.'

Women just like Mary and Alison came forward in their hundreds to help the exhausted and hungry men. Some of the soldiers had not eaten or drunk for four or five days.

By 29th May the county had been virtually ransacked to provide food and clothing for the troops. Collection centres were set up at Tonbridge, Faversham and Headcorn. In Margate the Dreamland Amusement Park was opened as a clothing store as was the Pavilion at Ramsgate. The shops of Dover were searched for belts and braces which could be used to hold up the army trousers which were available.

Frank Howard of Ramsgate had his wardrobe ransacked by his wife Olive and ended up with no shoes, socks, handkerchiefs, shirts or underwear. She made her own sacrifice, badly blistering her hands cutting loaves and making sandwiches so they had to be bandaged for some time.

Many firms donated food and clothing, and everybody did something to help. In Ramsgate an appeal was made over the local Redifusion radio service as Mary Cannon remembers:

'We appealed on the local Redifusion asking the residents of Thanet for any bread, cheese, eggs, anything we could feed the troops with, without having to cook it. We had food right up to the ceiling, bread, nothing else but loaves of bread.'

As troops were now landing at local ports in their thousands, it was essential that they were moved on as quickly as possible. Southern Railway provided trains and drivers especially for this purpose and special services were laid on to take the troops away from Kent to rejoin their Regiments.

Trains were allowed to stop for up to twenty minutes to allow more food and cups of tea to be passed through to the hungry soldiers. It was at the railway stations that the women of the WVS came into their own. The Women's Voluntary Service, with the help of the Military and numerous other volunteers, allowed thousands of soldiers to get their first decent meal in days. In Headcorn, for example, a large barn near the station was turned into a catering headquarters and the food prepared entirely by volunteers was taken across a field as the trains pulled into the station. A similar system was in operation at Paddock Wood, Faversham and other stopping points throughout the county.

The carriage doors of the trains had been locked so food and drink was passed through the open windows. Post cards and scraps of paper were given out so troops could write a scribbled note to their families letting them know they were safe.

Gladys Wilber commuted between Tonbridge and London during the war and clearly remembers the scene at Tonbridge station:

'There were long trestle tables on the platforms and as the trains came in they handed the men sandwiches and cakes and tea, it was marvellous really, and all of the men in the trains were waving letters saying, "Will you post this," probably to families, mothers or wives. We all took them and posted them, handfuls of them. It was really incredible, the spirit of everybody helping, everybody friendly and anything one can do, one did, it was really good.'

Children too helped the soldiers, arranging door to door collections of food and clothing and helping at the stations. Although the docks area in Dover had been closed to the general public for the duration of the evacuation, Geoff Tinley knew the area well enough and knew exactly where to go to get a good view of what was going on. What he saw shocked him.

With Dunkirk came the realisation that war was not a game and scenes that met Geoff's young eyes at Dover have remained with him all his life:

'Because some of them coming up through the town were in a pretty poor state, we used to rush around and get bread and things from the shops just to give to them. Even at that age I remember thinking, well if this is war, what is yet to come? It really was a salutary lesson for youngsters as up until then we all thought it was great fun.'

As a teenager in Ramsgate, Vera Ferris can remember going around the houses. 'I knocked on people's doors to collect blankets and old sheets. There

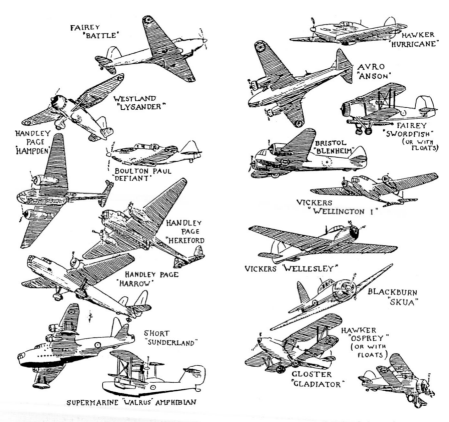

FAIREY 'BATTLE'

HAWKER 'HURRICANE'

AVRO 'ANSON'

WESTLAND 'LYSANDER'

FAIREY 'SWORDFISH' (OR WITH FLOATS)

HANDLEY PAGE 'HAMPDEN'

BRISTOL 'BLENHEIM'

BOULTON PAUL 'DEFIANT'

VICKERS 'WELLINGTON I'

HANDLEY PAGE 'HEREFORD'

VICKERS 'WELLESLEY'

HANDLEY PAGE 'HARROW'

BLACKBURN 'SKUA'

SHORT 'SUNDERLAND'

HAWKER 'OSPREY' (OR WITH FLOATS)

GLOSTER 'GLADIATOR'

SUPERMARINE 'WALRUS' AMPHIBIAN

Illustrations from the National Defence Pocket Book issued to all, whether in the Navy, Army, Air Force or Civilian Services. (L. Page)

was a place you took all the stuff, coats and jumpers, anything that was going to be of use to the troops being brought back. I thought I was doing great, I was sixteen and that was my bit towards the war.'

Brenda Keatley's father was working for the railway and knew in advance that the troops would be returning. She recalls:

'When they came in they gave them those iron ration dog biscuits which even the dogs wouldn't eat. Some of the men hadn't got any clothes but they clutched their rifles, they were not allowed to let their rifles go. Once the local people got to know they brought clothes, old clothes, but they would sew buttons on and get everything ready.

'The bakers took bread, my mother took stuff, but she didn't let us round, she thought it was too sad for us to see. Those poor men, there was nothing for them. It was really sad.'

Bessie Newton, whose father worked in Dover Docks, recalls his reaction. 'Dad in fact worked on the pier. He was so upset because he'd helped to get them off the boats with the injured. He had served in the First World War as a very young man, he went under-age in fact, and it brought back memories for him. He couldn't say much, he was so overwhelmed by the suffering of those men and also he mentioned how brave and cheerful they were, in spite of everything.'

As a child Vicki Graham used to take refreshments in a basket to a local crossing in Ashford. At first she said: 'I didn't realise that the men lying exhausted in the trains were soldiers at all, all I remember are these tired men and blankets and things. I think it reminded me of my father. He lost his eye and war had always held a certain significance for me and here it was at first hand, you know, men who had been in a war.'

The returning troops made a similar impression on Colin Cuthbert:

'I saw some very shattered demoralised men literally with hardly any clothes on just walking about Margate harbour not knowing where they were going. I can remember that quite vividly as a young man.'

The Dunkirk spirit was certainly to the fore in Ramsgate where, like many women, Mary Cannon set to work preparing food and drink for the soldiers. She worked for eight days without a break, until the last of the ships had returned, and survived on only two hours sleep a night. Along with other volunteers, she slept on the stage of the Theatre Royal. She takes up her story:

'Every day my mother used to bring me down clean clothing. We couldn't have a bath, there were no baths there. We took one of the little dressing rooms and took bowls to have a wash down.'

Mary recalls it was on the second day of the evacuation that the people of Ramsgate realised the soldiers' hunger and thirst and the spirit of enterprise came to the rescue.

'We could boil eggs but we didn't have enough hands to do any real cooking, there weren't any plastic cartons for margarine or butter so they just came in ordinary wrappings with tins of corned beef, tins of salmon — very few of those but there were some. One of us had the idea of going to a local butcher's which was also a cold meat shop to hire a bacon slicer which was not electrically driven, you had to use your hands for it. Well, it saved your hands from blistering against the old carving knife.

'Towards the end I think we got sick to death of seeing loaves of bread, but we did make the troops sandwiches. Then, of course, there was the question of drinking. We didn't have a hundred cups in our little café so we put out another Redifusion appeal for cups, even if they were chipped or without handles, as many cups as possible we needed. In the end we even had jam jars, we kept making and making and making tea, we ran out of milk one day. We appealed for tinned milk, any sort of milk, because you couldn't get dried milk in those days.'

As well as feeding the men, Mary and her fellow workers did something for the soldiers' morale. She continues:

'A soldier asked us on the pier if we could send a letter off for him. He gave us the letter to send and gave us all the idea of going round to the different stationery shops in Ramsgate appealing for postcards, any postcards. We wrote on the cards, "arrived safely in England" and then we would take them up to the top of the pier where the soldiers were coming in with pens and pencils and they got passed along the pier and then we collected the written postcards from the soldiers. I've no idea how many we sent, but our staff were only getting a couple of hours sleep at the Royal Pavilion. In twenty-four hours we were on the go continuously, all the time.'

The successful evacuation of so many men from the beaches of Dunkirk owed much to the weather. The overcast skies and frequent rainstorms of the preceding few days had prevented a number of enemy aircraft attacks but 30th May dawned bright and clear and the Luftwaffe began attacking the beaches, now black with men, with renewed enthusiasm.

Reg Cutting, as a twenty-five-year old with the Royal Army Service Corps, had to wait for two days and two nights on the beaches of La Panne before being directed out to the water's edge. He soon discovered the worst was yet to come.

'At dusk we went down to the water's edge where we were lined up in tiers, in sixes with arms linked. There was an Officer there with a revolver, and nobody was allowed to rush and we waited until a boat appeared in the dimness from out at sea somewhere, then we advanced in the water, the whole column moving until we were up to our waists. The boat took six on board because it was a rowing boat and couldn't carry any more. It went out a little further to the Margate Lifeboat and put the first six on board, ferried back and forth like that until the lifeboat had enough on board to move out to the Dutch ship. We went up a scramble net and then down into the hold. You just sat down exhausted and thankful.'

For every soldier that was rescued, others were forced to wait behind and await their turn. Some like Leslie Page began to doubt if they would ever see their home again. He describes the scene:

'Washing up on the beach were the dead bodies of the men who were killed from the ships that had just been sunk and you had a weird feeling that you were all in this, but would you get out of it? How would you get out of it? There was no way that you could, you sat there and thought England's across there, your home is across there, it's only across the Channel, yet how are you going to get out? All the shelling going on and the machine gunning and the men running around. I remember a church service on the beach, we all sat there or knelt there praying hoping that you would get a boat that wasn't going to get sunk or bombed.'

Jack Sharp, a signalman on the mine sweeper *Nankoe,* was working from the first day evacuating men:

'The Navy didn't have a phoney war. We'd seen action since 3rd September 1939 but Dunkirk beat everything. It was terrible. Some men were wounded, most shocked. We gave them the usual naval routine of cocoa and corned beef sandwiches, easy for our cooks to make. I don't recall rum being mentioned. They were wet and cold and we emptied our stores of jerseys, duffel coats, trousers, uniforms, whatever was needed.'

Major Cyril Innis helped to load the wounded from the Dunkirk beaches:

'We took a stretcher and took the chaps to the quay and put them on this minesweeper. Some were too bad to walk, they had various wounds to their arms and legs. As we were putting them on the minesweeper a destroyer, the *Wakefield* I think, told us to get going as there was a submarine in the area. About four minutes later there was a terrible explosion, with hundreds of chaps in the water. We must have taken 200 of them on board.'

On 31st May the evacuation of allied troops from the beaches of Dunkirk reached its peak. Sixty-eight thousand troops were safely brought across the Channel but of the thirty-four thousand soldiers who landed at Dover over a thousand were badly injured. The authorities realised that the number of wounded personally requiring immediate medical attention was also about to reach its peak.

An appeal for extra nurses to come forward had been made after the six o'clock news the night before, for trained women to join the Civil Nursing Reserve. Nurses had already been drafted to Kent, from top London hospitals, Guy's and St Thomas', to tend the injured and dying.

Information about the number of wounded on any one ship coming into port was broadcast over a loud speaker system and a medical officer and two sick berth ratings would board the vessel to ascertain the number of casualties.

Nora Doughty was a member of the Margate Ambulance Service:

'We could hear them being told on the loud hailer across the sea how many casualties there were, how many first aid, how many walking, how many dead, so the people this end with the ambulances knew exactly what to expect.'

Joan Rootes remembers the fish market in Margate being boarded up and used for stretcher cases.

Gwen Devereux remembers the Winter Gardens as a reception centre and Dreamland as a first aid post. The worst cases were taken to Margate General or to the Royal Sea Bathing Hospital.

Fred Gore saw wounded men taken to the Pleasure Centre in Ramsgate:

'There were terrible sights. I saw men with half their body blown away, I saw what the undertaker had to deal with. There is a special memorial to

Lewis Gun—*continued.*

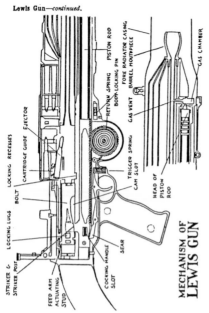

MECHANISM OF LEWIS GUN

Lewis Gun—*continued.*

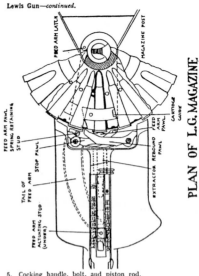

PLAN OF L.G. MAGAZINE

back to disengage from pinion casing. Allow pinion casing to drop so that pinion is not engaged and draw back c.h. far enough to give the decrease wanted. With left hand press up pinion casing to engage rack with pinion and slide forward pistol grip, when c.h. will fly forward. Test.

Stripping and Assembling.

Place parts in clean place in rotation, and assemble in reverse order. **Body Group.**

1. Butt. See that the cocking handle is forward.
2. Body Cover. See that the feed-arm is over to the right.
3. Feed Arm.
4. Pinion casing. Do not withdraw pistol grip completely.

5. Cocking handle, bolt, and piston rod.
6. Pistol grip, body locking pin, and body.
   Barrel Group.
1. Clamp ring and front radiator casing. No. 2 screw only .r to be unscrewed as far as to bring it flush with outside of left wing of clamp ring.
2. Field Mount (if used).
3. Gas regulator and key.
4. Rear radiator casing. Slide off to rear.
5. Gas cylinder. When using piston rod as wrench, take care not to fracture rear end of gas cylinder.
6. Gas chamber.
7. Barrel mouthpiece. Do not forget that it has a left-handed thread. **Components.**
   Only the following components will be stripped. Others may be stripped only by instructors or armourers.
   Cartridge guide. Magazine stop pawls. Feed arm pawl and spring. Pinion group, less pinion pawl. Extractor. Take care not to strain it by pushing it outwards more than needed. Ejector.

More illustrations from the National Defence Pocket Book.   (L. Page)

them in Ramsgate cemetery for the English and foreigners who came back from Dunkirk but did not survive.'

The majority of wounded were taken to hospitals around the county and indeed throughout the country as swiftly as possible.

Rene Spellward, a thirteen-year-old living in Tunbridge Wells, recalls:

'I remember seeing lots of Red Cross trains bringing the injured back from Dunkirk. The trains had massive red crosses painted on the top and you would see the military Red Cross ambulances going to take the troops to the local hospital. Those that could walked up, some on crutches and some with head bandaged and that was rather a tear-jerker.'

Beds were made available not only in regular hospitals but also in mental institutions. Ursula Hall-Thompson joined the Red Cross as a VAD after leaving school. During Dunkirk her role was to assist the fully trained doctors and nurses in the operating theatre. She was sent to a military hospital near Dover where at the height of the emergency three operations were taking place within the theatre at once.

'All the time there were patients coming in who were taken off the boats and who were too desperately ill to go any further. Most of the army people went inland on hospital trains and we had the people who were dying or who would die if they did not have immediate treatment.

'Patients came into the operating theatre and were mostly amputations because they all had tourniquets over the other side and you shouldn't leave a tourniquet on for more than five minutes but they'd had them on for a day or two so there was a great deal of gangrene.'

A motel on the promenade at La Panne to the east of Dunkirk had been fitted out as a military hospital by the Belgian authorities and the Royal Army Medical Corps who had taken it over did their best to treat the wounded with limited supplies of medical and surgical equipment. Ironically those who were thrown into the sea, thereby exposing their wounds to long periods in salt water, were less likely to need limbs amputated when they eventually reached hospital, as the salt water had speeded up the healing process. The pressure on the medical staff at home continued to mount and they found they had an additional problem to cope with, fatigue. Ursula Hall-Thompson was herself working on an eight hour shift, eight hours on, eight hours off, for the full ten days of the evacuation and she noticed the pressure was also beginning to tell on her colleagues, although there were some unorthodox solutions to this problem.

'We left one desperately ill patient behind with an orderly to look after him, and the orderly had quite a sense of humour. I asked him how he managed to keep awake when he had to sit with the patient and the orderly said, "Oh I gave him a walking stick and I lay on the bed next to him and said to him "if you feel worse give me a poke with your walking stick". This poor man was practically dying and that wasn't going to be very helpful but still there you are.'

Martyn Down was a fourteen-year-old in the Emergency Hospital Service, and he served in the West Kent Hospital in Maidstone and also with St John's Ambulance Brigade in the town. These young men were really employed as messengers but in practice they did anything — manning switchboards, stretcher bearing, whatever was necessary at the time. During the Dunkirk evacuation casualties came into Maidstone. Martyn continues his story:

'One morning there was a call to say a convoy of badly wounded personnel was on its way from the coast. They arrived by converted coaches which held twelve stretcher cases, two and three deep down the bus. They were loaded off through the central emergency door at the back of the hospital.

'They had come from the coast in the charge of VAD nurses and the coaches had been converted by the Maidstone and District and East Kent Road Car Company. When the soldiers arrived they were in pretty bad condition. They weren't straight out of the water but had been treated down on the coast. All had been vomiting badly on the journey from the coast due to the jolting of the vehicle and also some medication they had received. Some stayed a few days in the ward before being moved on, some of course died, but the worst ones were those who had been in the burning oil caused by ships being torpedoed and bombed and split open. The poor chaps were immersed in oil so they were burnt from head to waist at least and in many cases, far worse. The dressings made them look like mummies with white bandaging or even plastering which encased the upper part of their bodies in order to retain the burn ointment which had been smeared all over them. They were a fearful sight as they just had splits in their plaster for their eyes, nose and mouth and had to be fed exclusively with feeding bottles. In particular I was extremely frightened at night because they were in a darkened ward in an old part of the hospital, with just a pale blue light shining in the ward and it was quite eerie to see all those poor chaps sitting up in bed, they must have been in absolute agony.'

By 1st June the whole of Britain was told about the 'Miracle of Dunkirk'. 'Tens of thousands safely home already, many more coming day by day', ran the headline in the 'Daily Express', while the 'Times' referred to the 'BEF's gallant fight' and mentioned the thousands of troops who had successfully been brought home to England.

The local Kent papers were circumspect in their coverage. The 'Dover Express' and the 'East Kent News', for example, reported that refugees were now a feature of life in Dover. Many had been bedded down at the Town Hall, including an eleven-year-old boy who had made his way, unaided, from Brussels. Other stories told of a small puppy only a few weeks old rescued from Dunkirk by one of the crew members of the gun boat, *Locust*, who feared that the dog was in danger of being trampled underfoot. The newspapers reported with glee that the puppy had now become the ship's mascot. What the reports of the time did not say however, was that hundreds of dogs who fled with their original owners from the advancing German armies had attached themselves to the soldiers waiting on the beaches to be rescued and the animals had managed to clamber aboard the ships. Many were badly injured, however, just like their human companions. Some were covered in oil and others had bullet wounds. The Dover RSPCA Inspector later reported that of the 176 dogs evacuated during the ten days, only thirty survived.

Every account of the evacuation, whether in the press or on the wireless, was carefully worded to ensure that no potentially valuable information was given away to the enemy. It was equally important to ensure that morale was in no way damaged by the reports.

The people of Kent who saw those men arrive for themselves remembered what the wireless reports and the newspaper stories of the day glossed over. Vicki Graham, a schoolgirl who had been evacuated to Kent remembers:

'I was at the railway line and these trains started to come through absolutely packed with men of all descriptions, soldiers, sailors, airmen. They were in all states of dress and undress, I think I was quite shocked in a way and of course they were all nationalities and what came through to me was their complete exhaustion. These were not smiling men, these were exhausted men. They were grey and so tired they were sleeping on their feet and I couldn't help wondering what on earth had happened to some of them and how they had come to be like this.'

What the newspaper reports also omitted to convey was that 1st June had been a black day for the allies. Three destroyers and many small craft had been lost in what turned out to be one of the Luftwaffe's most successful raids. At Government level there was also much criticism of the RAF and its Commanding Officer, Air Chief Marshall Sir Hugh Dowding, whom it was felt should be doing more to speed up the evacuation by thwarting the Luftwaffe's now frequent attacks. He insisted on preserving his pilots and his planes for the battle that he was sure was to come, the Battle of Britain. From now on the troops would have to be evacuated from the beaches at night and time was running out.

Jack Sharp who was serving with the Royal Navy at the time of Dunkirk recalls the role of the RAF somewhat differently:

'I would like to say that the RAF were there. They employed 16 squadrons over the whole evacuation area, 111 patrols and 4,822 flying hours. The official figure apparently agreed by the Germans was that 265 planes were destroyed. I think the RAF deserve some credit and I want to shoot down this story about no RAF being there at all.'

The need to evacuate as many fit men as possible became overwhelming and it was reluctantly decided that the stretcher cases would have to be left behind because they were taking up too much room aboard the ships. As it became increasingly evident that some men would have to be left behind, not unnaturally a wave of panic swept through the remaining soldiers. Although in some areas the evacuation still continued in an orderly fashion, in many others confusion and fear reigned as men scrambled aboard the nearest waiting ship or raft or held onto the tow rope still carrying their rifles and clothed in heavy army great coats now sodden with water and oil. Many of the little ships overturned because of the sheer number of men aboard, causing further panic, but even in the midst of all this chaos many of the soldiers retained their sense of humour as Roger Bellamy recalls:

'I saw a very tall ginger-haired soldier about six foot two or three, a massive fellow, with a diminutive Padre on his shoulders wading out to sea. We all

John Curley in his Royal Army Service Corps uniform before being sent to France in January 1940. (J. Curley)

heard the Padre say, "Courage my son, the Lord is with us, the Lord is with us," and the soldier said, "He'd better be mate, or I'm going to drop you."'

Another humorous incident was recalled by William Hewitt:

'We were involved with rescuing the Third Battalion of the Grenadier Guards at La Panne. They were being rescued at midnight and being guards, lined up on the beach waiting for orders to embark. It was getting light and the bombing had started. The two army pontoons, heavy vessels with canvas sides and loaded with guards with all their equipment, buckets and all sorts of things, were a heavy tow. One of the pontoons capsized and we had to go back and haul the chaps out of the water. We rescued the majority but we simply couldn't lift this other chap aboard, he had all his equipment but no rifle and turned out to be their Quartermaster. We had to make a rope fast round his armpits and tow him behind the motorboat with the survivors on this pontoon. It took five stokers to lift him up onto the deck of the ship. One of the stewards inquired where to put him and I said, "In my cabin," because he had been the largest fish I'd landed. He weighed twenty-two stone. He was not in a very good state and his face was blue and awful as he had taken in a lot of water. In any event he was put in my bunk and we continued with the job of getting back to Dover.

'The next morning at 5.00 am we were sailing back to Dunkirk when I remembered he was in my bunk. I couldn't do anything about it so I went down and said to him, "I'm terribly sorry, but I'm afraid you're on your way back again." He was delighted and said, "I'll meet my chums, I'm very glad to hear that. Only one thing please, could you get me back my jacket?" At that time he was wearing a soldier's general service jacket, not a battledress, and we had stuck it in the boiler room to dry. I sent the steward to find it and when it arrived the Quartermaster put his hand in the inner pocket and pulled out the biggest wadge of white fivers I have ever seen. The entire mess funds of the Third Battalion of the Grenadier Guards. This led to quite a few parties I attended with him.'

By 3rd June exhaustion was beginning to affect the men whose responsibility it was to bring the troops back safely into England. For nine days and nine nights without rest, the Royal Navy and the little ships had ploughed back and forth across the Channel without a thought for their own safety. Many local life boats had played a particularly important role in the evacuation.

As a result, Howard Knight, the Coxswain of the Ramsgate lifeboat, *Prudential*, and Edward Parker, the Coxswain of the Margate lifeboat, *Lord Southborough*, were both awarded the 'Distinguished Service Medal' for their gallantry and determination. The staff of Southern Railway took responsibility for transporting the soldiers away from Kent and laid on over 2,000 locomotives and carriages for this purpose. It was a distressing experience for drivers such as Charles Griffin because the situation at the ports was often confused and the soldiers were locked into the carriages to prevent them escaping, especially when they were under pressure towards the end of the evacuation. Charles Griffin recalls:

'There were soldiers on the platform and on the tracks and before we could run into number four Reception Road they had to clear all the soldiers out of the way and that took some long time to do.'

Despite these problems, the people of Kent never tired in their efforts to help the soldiers. Apart from the veritable army of volunteers, individuals throughout the county were trying to make the evacuation that much easier and quicker in the final twenty-four hours. The Chief Constructor at Sheerness Dockyard built a number of small rafts while local shipwrights made rope ladders to enable the soldiers to scramble onto the large naval vessels more easily.

Nothing could be done about the equipment which littered the French beaches. The British Army lost half a million tons of military stores and ammunition and two thousand guns, and nearly every one of the tanks taken over to France. Although much was set on fire and destroyed by the retreating allied forces, there was still potentially enough equipment for two German armoured divisions.

Roger Bellamy from Folkestone describes his actions:

'We had to leave our machine guns in Dunkirk but as a little parting gift we placed hand grenades under each leg of the tripod.'

The feelings of those soldiers who did get away on that final day were mixed. For the French and Belgian refugees who had fought beside the British troops, there were feelings of despair and bitterness as they left their homeland behind. On arriving in England, many threw the few French coins they possessed from the train windows in disgust. Their feelings were shared by many British soldiers. John Howarth from Wainscott, realising that the evacuation of Dunkirk was a retreat and not a victory, could not believe the reception given to a defeated army by the people of Ramsgate.

'It was unbelievable, it really was, I couldn't thank them enough, I can never thank them enough. "Nice to see you home," they said with tears in their eyes, I was choked.'

John Curley has equally vivid memories of that time.

'Before we got to Dover my feelings and the feelings of many of us, I'm sure, were of shame. We felt degraded, we were really at rock-bottom, at zero. We couldn't believe what had happened to us, we thought that we were the British Army retreating from the Continent which had never happened before like that and we were ashamed to death. We didn't want to meet the people of Dover, we didn't want to meet the people of anywhere on the coast because we were frightened that they would simply throw stones at us. That is what I imagined. We came into Dover and I thought "Oh God, we've got to face all this now". When we arrived in Dover they put the gang-planks on board and we came down to the most magnificent reception I've ever seen in my life. The ladies of Dover and all the people of Dover itself were clapping and cheering us and we couldn't believe this because we'd lost, we'd been kicked out of France by a really efficient German Army. We couldn't believe that these people were welcoming us home again like this. What they did for our morale, boosted it right to the top I can assure you, I thought with people like this behind us, how the hell can we lose the war? And if the Germans had invaded us there and then I feel sure we would have fought them with our bare hands, we felt that good having landed in Dover.

'And when we left Dover and went up to London, the tracks, the whole seventy miles of it was still lined by these people on both sides, clapping and cheering us. Every time we stopped there was tea thrust at us, cakes, all sorts of things, you would have thought we were a conquering army instead of a defeated one. I can't thank those people enough for restoring us to sanity.'

One of the last people to be evacuated from the Dunkirk beaches was George Sone who spent the night of the 3rd and 4th June waiting to be rescued. He describes the beach as hell. A hospital ship had been bombed, he saw British planes, injured soldiers, bullet wounds and shrapnel. He was so tired he cannot even remember the crossing, he simply remembers being woken up at Dover and being rushed on to a train. He retells his story:

'I woke up at the first stop which was Sittingbourne and I tried to get out of the train but I couldn't. Every train door was locked, we were prisoners, we had nothing to eat or drink and there I was in my home town. I just managed to drop a piece of paper out as a message for my parents to say I was alive. I wrote my mother's name and address and my message, "I'm safe, George." She was finally brought that message by the stationmaster.'

Betty Harden, a schoolgirl from Ashford, saw a moving moment on the railway crossing:

'I remember a woman saw her husband on the train. She scrambled up the embankment and was able to kiss him, but then the train moved on, but at least she knew he was safe, although I don't know how long it was before she heard from him.'

At 9.00 am on 4th June 1940 General Beaufrere, on behalf of the Allies, surrendered the town of Dunkirk into enemy hands. 'Operation Dynamo' was over, although sixty vessels were still to unload their cargo of men at Dover and the last train eventually left the town at four o'clock that afternoon.

Some men at the end of their ordeal celebrated with quite ordinary comforts. Bob Viney of the Royal Artillery was taken from Dover to Derby where he remained for two weeks before re-joining his regiment. He remembers:

'They gave us writing paper to let us write home. On the following day the Mayor of Derby came out and gave a razor, a shaving brush and five shillings to every one of us.'

For the people of Kent, the end of the evacuation brought a grave realisation that a Nazi invasion was now a very real possibility. All signposts in the county had been taken down, all milestones uprooted and the names of the streets removed or obliterated in an attempt to confuse the enemy. The coastal towns became like ghost towns as people afraid of a possible invasion moved further inland. Sheep and cattle were evacuated from Romney Marsh.

It was in the days following Dunkirk that tributes were paid to the bravery of the Navy, the Air Force and all who had manned the 'Armada' of little ships.

By the time the evacuation was over, the crews of the cross-Channel boats had earned seven Distinguished Service Crosses, two Distinguished Service Medals and six Mentions in Despatches, but no medals were awarded by the British Government to the Dunkirk veterans or indeed those men who fought so bravely for over ten days ensuring that the Dunkirk perimeter remained intact for the duration of the evacuation. Many of those men gave their lives or were taken prisoner.

Dunkirk was a miracle, not a victory. Over 300,000 men were evacuated from the beaches and the Government had expected no more than 45,000 to make it back to England. A total of 68,000 men were lost along with the guns, motor vehicles and ammunition, a total of 243 ships had been sunk, including six British Destroyers. The RAF lost 474 aircraft. It was a defeat of gigantic proportions, but Winston Churchill realised in one of his most famous speeches, that it was no use looking at past defeats, England had to look to the future, the Battle of Britain was about to begin. The people of Kent who had tasted their first experience of real war during Dunkirk were now to endure the experience which earned the County the nickname 'Bomb Alley'.

Damage to houses in Blenheim Road, Deal, during the first serious raid in the town on Sunday 18th August 1940.   (M. Kirkaldie)

Joyce Bishop at home in Dartford. Adhesive tape to avoid flying glass proved useless when a bomb fell on Princes Road.

(J. Bishop)

Chapter VIII
THE BATTLE OF BRITAIN

The end of August 1940 marked the beginning of the critical period of the Battle of Britain. The Luftwaffe turned their attention away from attacking merchant shipping and radar installations to concentrate on Britain's front line airfields. The aim was simple: to crush the RAF's defensive capabilities and establish air superiority before staging an invasion of the United Kingdom. This became known as Operation Sealion.

Air Chief Marshall Sir Hugh Dowding, in charge of RAF Fighter Command, had the unenviable task of defending Britain from the might of the well equipped and highly trained German Air Force. Four of Kent's airfields played a vital role in that defence: Manston, Hawkinge, Gravesend and Biggin Hill. The two airfields at Eastchurch and Detling were used by Coastal Command, who had the task of detecting preparations for an invasion or, in an emergency, by the fighter pilots when their planes were badly damaged. Lympne was also available for use in emergencies but West Malling, badly bombed in an air raid on 10th August, was unable to accept its first Squadron of Spitfires until late October. These airfields were a part of Number 11 Group Fighter Command under the jurisdiction of Air Vice Marshall Keith Park.

In 1940, as the nearest land mass to occupied Europe, Kent was often said to have changed from being 'The Garden of England' to 'The Guardian'. Her people saw more enemy action than any other county in the British Isles, for when the German bombers failed to find their target they aimed their bombs at the nearest centres of population. This was exactly what happened on 24th August when Ramsgate suffered its worst air raid of the war. A raid on RAF Manston at lunch time left seventeen people dead and three badly damaged aircraft. The airfield was put out of action for several hours as a bomb had severed telephone and teleprinter circuits. Living quarters had also been destroyed and the presence of a number of unexploded bombs made the evacuation of all administrative and ground staff essential. The destruction was so widespread that within minutes the airfield was obscured by smoke and dust, making it impossible for a second wave of enemy bombers to see their target. They dropped their bombs instead on Ramsgate, killing thirty-one people and seriously injuring fifty-four others. It was the town's highest death toll of the war.

Fred Gore remembers the raid well:

'I saw a gentleman standing at Dunne's Furniture Store looking up at the sky. A bomb came and blew him to pieces. I was up near the Queen Street entrance when that bomb fell. He was blown to bits and his shoes were found in the market place at Ramsgate.'

The gas works were also hit and put out of action. As a result the town had no gas or water for twelve days.

During the raid many of the inhabitants fled to the air raid tunnels under nearby cliffs. Some people were so frightened they chose to live there, sleeping on bunk beds and cooking on small oil stoves.

Vera Ferris's mother did the same, but on 24th August she decided to return home to cook her husband's lunch. It was a decision which nearly cost her her life.

'The sirens had gone and we were all down the tunnel. It had been quiet and there were no planes going over so my mother just decided to go home and cook my father's dinner. The air raid warden at the top of the tunnel said, "You shouldn't go home, you should stop down the tunnel." "Oh no," she said, "It's quiet, I'm going home." So off she went down Bellevue Road and almost at the bottom she heard the planes coming over and she didn't know what to do, whether to go back to the tunnel or to go home. She decided it was quicker to go home. Luckily she didn't choose to use the back way which we would normally use when coming from the tunnel. Had my mother done that — why she didn't I don't know, except possibly the planes coming over unnerved her — she would have been killed instantly.'

During the long, hot, summer of 1940 the Spitfires and Hurricanes of Fighter Command were all that stood between Hitler and total victory. Despite the fact that the Hurricane was credited with destroying more enemy aircraft than the Spitfire, it was the Spitfire which became universally popular. It was a joy to fly and many pilots felt they had developed a very special relationship with the plane, as Wing Commander Paddy Barthropp remembers:

'It was the greatest thing that man ever produced. It was a beautiful, manoeuvrable plane with eight machine guns and fairly good visibility. It flew weil and was reliable. We used to talk to it. Coming back here one day I was shot up and wondered if I'd make land at Folkestone or on the beach. I'd say, "Just a little bit further and we'll make it," and it always did.'

Stan Walton from Canterbury agreed:

'If you analyse the Battle of Britain, Hurricanes did three-quarters of the work and the Spitfires a quarter. The Spitfires had the glamour. It was a pretty, almost a beautiful aeroplane.'

With so many planes being destroyed there was a widespread fear that the RAF did not have enough planes or enough qualified pilots to defend the British Isles successfully. Each plane had to be handled with care as Jimmy Corbin remembers:

'If you damaged it through bad flying or carelessness, that was bad enough. For instance, some people came in and forgot to put their undercarriage down. If it was their fault and not a technical fault, then they were really reprimanded for it.'

Despite the obvious dangers there was no discounting the attraction of becoming a pilot with Fighter Command to many men during the war, as former pilot Stan Walton recalls:

'When you pass your Wings and they ask you what you want to do, be a fighter pilot or a bomber, you immediately say fighter pilot. Then some brash interviewer says, "Well what the hell, can't you take responsibility for the crew?".

'Then they realise that is your aim, to be a fighter pilot. It's an individual job, you make your own decisions and you don't have to consider making a silly decision and risking somebody else's life. If you make a silly decision, you're only risking your own. That may be considered a lack of responsibility, I don't know, but to me it was the fact that it gave me the opportunity to express myself.'

Paddy Barthropp was nineteen years of age and saw himself as an officer in the RAF, getting paid to do a job:

'I was trained before the war. Luckily I had had four or five hundred hours of flying when the Battle of Britain started, so I was a reasonably experienced pilot for those days. Some had only one hundred hours' experience in an aeroplane. If they survived the first three or four weeks they usually got away with it. A pilot's day often started as early as 8.00 am and did not end until well into the evening. There were inevitably long periods of waiting around, waiting for the call to take off or scramble. This was often the worst part of the job for many pilots.

'I was terrified, until you actually got into your aeroplane and you started climbing to wherever you were climbing, then you were alright. But the initial fright was when the telephone rang in the dispersal room and the adrenalin ran a bit. But I enjoyed every minute of it until I was shot down, eventually, and put in a prison camp.'

Over three hundred fighter pilots were lost during the Battle of Britain. As former pilot Jimmy Corbin remembers, men often waited in vain, sometimes hours at a time, for their friends to return:

'They used those horrible phrases like "poor old so and so has gone for a Burton", or "so and so hasn't come back". You used to hang around and hope that the telephone would go some time and say he'd bailed out or crash landed. Eventually you would have the horrible news that he wasn't coming back and there was no use sitting down and crying about these things, it was one of the things you had to put up with, a day to day occurrence.'

Ron Allen at the door of the sleeping accommodation for the Searchlight Troop HQ at Scrapsgate, Isle of Sheppey. During the Battle of Britain he was machine-gunned on that spot but the Germans missed him — but only just!   (R. Allen)

Phil Gilham in full flying gear at Detling airfield.   (J. Gilham)

Pilots like Stan Walton had accepted that their lives would be short and just got on with the job:

'We knew it might be a short life so what the hell, why not make it a merry life so off duty you did make it a merry life and that's it.'

The risks did not stop young men from wanting to join the Royal Air Force. Stan Walton remembers:

'The glamour began from the moment you started your training and there was a little white flash in your cap, everyone knew you were training to be air crew and you were put on a small pedestal. When you finally got your Wings everyone saw because you always had to wear uniform. It was natural for young men in those days, they loved the panache the job brought. The silk scarf we wore was not just a matter of glamour, it had a very useful purpose.

'A fighter pilot needed to keep his eyes continually open, not just in front but all the way round, behind him as well, so he is continually swivelling his

136

head. It would chafe quite a bit on an ordinary tunic or flying jacket collar if you didn't have something nice and soft around your neck.'

Support provided by the Civil Defence Network was invaluable, although decidedly less glamorous than the life of an RAF pilot. This was particularly true of the Observer Corps, later the Royal Observer Corps. At the onset of war in 1939, a network of observer posts country wide had been set up employing usually middle-aged civilian men who sent information by phone on the height, direction and strength of the enemy bombers as well as the type of aircraft. This information was then passed on to the nearest Fighter Command station so that the RAF could scramble its squadrons. It is often said that the wartime Observer Corps became the eyes and ears of the RAF taking over where radar left off. There was some form of rudimentary training but most of the men taught themselves aircraft recognition through cigarette cards or trade magazines. Reg Chambers was a member of the Observer Corps and like many others held down a full time job as well. From his post at Ham Hill near Snodland he covered the area which extended between Bearsted and Cobham. The facilities at the post were extremely basic:

'We had a hut where we used to boil our tea, we had an outside toilet which amounted to about forty acres and it was all outdoors because you couldn't plot an aeroplane in the dark. You looked through a type of telescope. You worked it around and as soon as it covered a number you knew where that particular plane was, and you could mark it on a map.'

Civilians also benefited from the information supplied by the Observer Corps because in effect they gave warning of an impending air raid. Olive Solomon was working at the headquarters of Dartford Rural Council in 1940 and was one of the people responsible for sounding the air raid siren:

'We used to get a call through from headquarters, wherever that might have been, giving us the alert which was an air raid warning red. There was a stand-down one and the siren warbled for a warning and a straight sound for the all clear. Whoever got there first did it.'

The sound of the siren would also alert the teams of local fire watchers on the look out for incendiary bombs. Martyn Down worked as a fire watcher on the roof of County Hall in Maidstone during the war:

'As soon as the air raid warning sounded we had to get up on the roof and remain alert with our equipment handy in anticipation of incendiary bombs falling. We had to know our way about on the roof and all the things you could fall over in the dark. As you went around you found people who perhaps had been up all night fire watching or in the Home Guard and then they had their normal work to do.

'Perhaps on their night we would have a continuous series of raids so it could happen that people were out on their feet through sheer exhaustion.'

Joan Clark worked as a telephonist for the Canterbury Civil Defence Controller in 1940 and despite difficult circumstances recognised the importance of her work:

'Mainly it was the telephone work, sending out the warnings to a lot of people; to wardens' posts, everyone who was connected with the approach of enemy aircraft. Doctors were concerned because they had to stay put while the raid was on, they weren't allowed to leave their surgeries unless they were needed. One midday when there was a very bad raid, Mother met with an accident which took her life. As far as I was concerned personally, I just went back to work in the afternoon straight after my mother's death.'

On 27th August 1940 Gillingham suffered its worst raid of the war. Just before midnight German bombers scored a direct hit on the bus station. Twenty people were killed and a further fifty injured. Beryl Moore remembers the raid: 'The ceilings started to crack, all the glass went everywhere from the ground outside. All the shop windows seemed to be coming out, it felt like an earthquake. As the all clear sounded in the early hours we put on warm clothing to go to see what had happened. Most people did, it was always a shock to see all the rubble and bricks and dust everywhere.'

This desire to see what was happening was shared by Joan Clark:

'I was part of a team of full time staff who sent out warnings as they came to us of the approaching aircraft. They also told us when the skies were clear again. We were working underground and really began to worry about what was going on outside because we couldn't hear shooting or machine guns or the planes coming down and yet we knew this was happening. We used to do, I think, a twelve hour shift from eight to eight, but sometimes the shift became erratic. They used the main council staff to help in the civil defence programme but they still had their own jobs to do. It was almost a twenty-four hour thing because we used to sleep on the premises in case we were needed. There were people coming and going all the time.'

One of Hitler's aims during the Battle of Britain, and also in the Blitz that followed, was to wear down civilian morale through the constant air raids. He under-estimated the will of the British people but he succeeded in worrying the Government. Throughout the war the Authorities made every effort to ensure that the general public did not become down-hearted. The importance of propaganda was recognised by both sides even down to giving inaccurate statements of the number of enemy bombers shot down. The majority of people believed what they were told, as Joan Clark recalls:

'The main thing was the news. You used to wait for the news on the wireless to know how many of our planes they had shot down or how many had come back to the airfield. I think that was the main topic on everyone's minds, you were always listening for news about the aircraft.'

Martyn Down remembers watching the planes:

'One did think of the pilots in particular. Quite specifically if those fellows didn't shoot them out of the skies we were going to be in dead trouble. It was always a very cheering experience though, to see a Spitfire going off into the distance doing a victory roll having shot down a victim.'

The Royal family and a number of key government ministers made frequent visits to towns and cities which had been devastated by raids. Winston Churchill visited RAF Manston and the town of Ramsgate on 28th August to see for himself the extent of the damage. He was reportedly appalled by what he saw. Nevertheless such visits were an important morale booster. Ordinary civilians also played their part in helping those in service. Gladys Townshend explains her contribution:

'During the Battle of Britain it was so hot that soldiers were allowed to have their shirts undone but only if they had a collar on their shirt. Some of them didn't and so I said, "Let me have one of your older shirts and I'll make you a collar." I cut the tail off and made a collar and it fitted very well. Then I think all the regiment brought all their shirts. I was so busy! They gave us little bits of rations in return, such as a tin of spam or something. You'd often find it wrapped up on the doorstep.'

Joan Ingram grew up on Kings Farm Estate during the war, not far from Gravesend airfield. 'My eldest brother was a paper boy up at the aerodrome and he would come home and tell Mum and Dad stories about the poor chaps saying they'd got nothing to do up there and that they were all lonely. He said to Mum, "Can't we throw a party for them?" So Mum and Dad used to throw a party and they just used to come down to unwind. We had a good time. We'd have a sing-song and a drink and smoke a cigarette, that was all.'

Olive Solomon, whose father-in-law was the local undertaker, lived near the station:

'The airmen used to come down from Gravesend airfield on their yellow bicycles and leave them here in our shed. We would have hundreds in there, and when they came back from leave they would come up from the station. Those that didn't have a bicycle would come and help themselves to one and ride back to the airfield, even though it didn't belong to them. When those that had left bicycles couldn't find one there was a bit of a fuss, so eventually we were put out of bounds.'

Civilians also needed assistance as Mary Smith from Eltham remembers:

'Everybody saw the funny side of everything they possibly could. My father was the postmaster and, like most younger people, was very inquisitive to know what was going on. One day he looked out to the square and saw an old lady strolling across with a terrible air battle going on overhead. She was carrying a jug with a whole lot of runner beans and was quite unaware of what was going on. My father grabbed her and made her sit and wait in the post office.'

As the battle reached its height, Kent's skies were often black with enemy aircraft as Ken Geering remembers:

'Hoards of German bombers were coming over. They often seemed so low that you could almost touch them. Like great big horrible black beetles protected by their fighters with our fighters trying to get in amongst them and shoot them down.'

Gladys Townshend describes how frustrating it was to watch helplessly from below. She was working in her garden at home in Goudhurst:

'I looked up and I could hear one of our planes up there on his own. I thought, "You silly man, you shouldn't be up there on your own," and all of a sudden there was an awful noise and from above him came two German Messerschmitts who fired on him. He came down in flames not far away, about a mile I thought from where we were living. So I got my Red Cross box, went on my bike and peddled away to where the crash was, thinking if he was hurt I could perhaps do something. He came down at Cherry Garden Farm and when we got there you couldn't do anything. He had nose dived into some cherry trees and was all on fire — you could see the poor pilot in there.'

Biddy Allen from Bilting was unable to give such practical help:

'You would hear the roar of the engines and you would see them spinning down and you'd shout, "Come on, out in your parachutes! Start jumping! Start jumping!" Of course usually they couldn't, although occasionally you did see a parachute floating down.'

As a young man living in Longfield Walter Bevan wanted to take a slightly more hands-on approach:

'You really had to take your hats off to the pilots, the discipline and the nerves — they were marvellous. The sky would look black with planes and I found it very frustrating just to stand on the ground and do nothing. I felt like getting a twelve bore out to shoot at them.'

All that could be seen of the dog fights in the skies above Kent were little dots and streamers trailing white cloudy vapour. But the noise was terrific, as Biddy Allen recalls:

'Another thing we would get were fighters fighting each other and I was standing on the door-step listening to the dog fight which you couldn't see. I heard the most incredible sound like a hail storm and wondered what it was. In fact it was the fighter diving and the bullets cutting the leaves off the trees. I'll never forget that, it was an extraordinary sound.'

Group Captain Tom Gleave clearly remembers the dog fight that he was involved in on 30th August 1940. On that day there was a devastating raid on Biggin Hill.

'In the afternoon I took up one flight and another chap took up another. I was leading and he suddenly went off to the left. He had seen what he thought was a raid of sorts. I followed and it was then that thirteen of these aircraft came down in front of me, they didn't see me so we drove into them straight away. That was a real old fashioned dog fight with everything tangled up like a ball of wool. I saw one plane literally tearing off the fabric and wood from the back of a Hurricane, an extraordinary sight. Eventually it was shot down. When I got back to Kenley there was this Hurricane sitting up on the tarmac looking like a herring after a cat has had supper. The old Hurricane was marvellous, it took enormous punishment.'

Margaret Collins from Maidstone remembers one lucky Spitfire pilot:

'The Battle of Britain took place right over our heads, throughout the late summer. I remember very vividly a German plane and a Spitfire flying over the house. Obviously the Spitfire had run out of ammunition. He was able to force the German down by getting very close to his tail and gradually he brought him down in a field not far away.'

Ursula Hall-Thompson worked as a mobile VAD with the Red Cross during the Battle of Britain. She was based for much of the time at Leeds Castle, which had been converted into a hospital:

'The Maiden's Tower had been turned into offices and a sterilising unit. In the castle itself we had three wards. One was the library. All the books were left there but boarded up with plywood. The stairways were boarded up as well, to stop the army boots wearing out the stone steps. Army beds and equipment were moved in. The patients used to play croquet on the lawn. We had about twenty or thirty patients, one surgical ward and two medical wards. We were quartered in their old staff rooms in the stables which were really quite comfortable.'

Her task in the operating theatre was to help the airmen to become fit enough to make the journey to the famous Queen Victoria Plastic and Jaw Injury Centre at East Grinstead. There they were treated for their burns by Sir Archibald McIndoe. The speed at which the medical staff worked was essential, as Ursula Hall-Thompson testifies:

'We used to say when we saw a plane come down, "We'll have a patient quite soon," and we used to turn on the sterilisers.'

Sir Archibald McIndoe has often been credited with giving the war injured from that period the will to live again and conquer their disability.

Eileen Dyke's father-in-law was one of Sir Archibald's guinea pigs, and had great respect for him and his nurses, as Eileen herself recalls:

Derek and Ken Hill aged seven and ten gave their mother Gladys a trying time in 1940 with their enthusiasm for collecting wartime souvenirs. (G. Townshend)

'There were some terrible cases of badly burned airmen. I don't know if this was actually true or not but I was told that all the pubs in East Grinstead turned their mirrors to the wall so that the poor fellows could not see how badly damaged they were. That is what Dad told me anyway.'

Group Captain Tom Gleave had reason to be grateful to the East Grinstead team. He was badly burned when he was shot down over Biggin Hill on 31st August 1940:

'I was set on fire and you would be surprised how quickly an aeroplane burns. By then we were at about 17,000 feet. I did everything to try and get out but the line was stuck for a while. If I pulled the big lever I'd have flown off but when you are being burnt you are a bit bemused. Eventually I got it undone and I just about opened the pilot canopy when she blew up completely. I went straight up in a sheet of flames. When the flames had gone away there was just me. There was no aircraft. I came down by parachute and landed in a field near a house called The Mace. I staggered to a gate where a farm labourer carried me on his back, gallant man, to this farmhouse and I was whisked into Orpington Hospital. I was very lucky because I was very badly burned, including all the skin on my legs and face. I was in Orpington for two months with excellent nursing, and then I was picked up by a chap called McIndoe and he took me to the Queen Victoria Hospital in East Grinstead. I spent a year there having plastic surgery and I was flying again in less than a year.'

The Women's Auxiliary Air Force, known as WAAFs, filled many important roles during the crucial months of the Battle of Britain. The women helped to ensure the smooth running of many behind the scenes operations at the Fighter Bases and Sector Stations as well as at Group Headquarters. They often worked as radar operators, plotters and filterers. Bunny Wareham from Coxheath served as a WAAF at Biggin Hill for much of the war. For girls still in their teens it was not an easy life:

'During the Battle of Britain we were on four watches and we each in turn did an eight hour shift. Then we would be relieved and we were expected to fit in our meals and our sleep accordingly. Usually we were in rooms of four or six girls together. Bathing was a bit difficult because there was always a shortage of hot water and we had to walk and go and get our meals in another house, which was taken over as a mess room. We were in the signals section and our job was to warn of approaching enemy aircraft. When this happened all our squadrons had to scramble and once they'd scrambled we were on tenterhooks waiting for them to come back. Often they would come back, refuel and have to go off again. It was a case of counting the numbers back all the time. This was particularly difficult when a girl happened to be friendly with one of the pilots.'

A number of WAAFs based at Hawkinge worked in what became known as the 'Y organisation'. Their job was to listen to German radio broadcasts and provide clues as to the Luftwaffe's aims, strengths and possible battle plans. Many of the men working at Hawkinge, including Doug Lee, a wireless operator, did not fully appreciate the work that the women did:

'We entertained these WAAFs from the Y section, they came to our mess and had their meals with us. Their officer in charge used to come along because I had a lot of stores under my wing and he would scrounge bits and pieces because he was still only in the early stages of building up an organisation. He said to me one day, "You'd be very useful in our organisation." I said to him, straight out, I suppose I shouldn't have looking back, but I said, "Well what exactly do you do?" He didn't reply. We knew vaguely what they were doing but not really, it was very hush hush.'

The Women's Auxiliary Air Force was a relatively young organisation in 1940. It had been formed a year earlier as a successor to the Women's Royal Flying Corps of World War I, which had in effect been disbanded in 1920. Because the presence of a woman on an airfield was still a relatively unusual sight in 1940, the WAAFs were frequently derided by their male colleagues. Those who worked in the Operations Room, for example, were often referred to as 'the Beauty Chorus'. Josie Fairclough, a WAAF at Detling, very quickly realised that the men did not have much regard for her at first:

'I think we were a bit of a novelty in the first instance and of course the regulars didn't go much on us, but I think even they came round eventually. Some people used to sew on a few buttons and that sort of thing.'

Another group of essential workers were the Ground Crew. No pilot could have got off the ground without their help, as former pilot Stan Walton explains:

'In our squadron we had the routine of taking our Ground Crew out once a week for a good binge because we felt that we owed that much to them anyway. If you had any sense as a pilot you made them your friends because you relied on them more than anyone or anything to have your aircraft in the condition which would bring you home again. I personally got on extremely well with my crew and I thought it paid dividends. It's all very well being a glamorous pilot but without those boys no pilot was any use at all.'

At the height of the battle it was not uncommon for pilots to take part in several sorties during the course of one day, only returning to the airfield to refuel. Many ground crews prided themselves on the speed in which they could complete their checks as Wilfred Dykes, a member of the Ground Crew at Hawkinge, recalls:

'From a squadron landing to a squadron being airborne again I think it was actually officially done in seven minutes, from the time the last one touched down to the first one being airborne. Check the petrol, oil, ammunition, oxygen bottles and plug in the starter trolley. This was a trolley with big batteries and a big lead going into the side of the engine. When the pilot was actually in the cockpit and ready to go he put his thumb up, you put your thumb up and pressed the button and that would start him off.'

After raids, priority was given to repairing any damage as quickly as possible so that the airfield was once again fully operational.

'Normally we got an air raid warning but invariably sometimes they were there before we even got the warning and all hell let loose. The first thing you knew was they were diving at you with a crunching of bombs and everybody running this way and that to get out of the way into a shelter. If you were on drome during a raid you had to get the aircraft away. If they were on the ground and we were there we would have them away in a couple of minutes.'

Charlie Wheeler's job was to fill in the bomb craters. He worked with eight other men and they divided their time between Hawkinge and Lympne airfields:

'You'd get hardcore and top soil, there was always plenty of that with the bombing around Folkestone. You picked it up and took it up to the site. There were no bulldozers then, it was all shovels. Then they brought a roller along and rolled it out as flat as they could and that was that. From a distance it looked like a lawn, it was lovely. When you got on it though there were bumps and lumps all over the place. The pilots must have had the feeling that the plane was going to tip over.'

Wilfred Dykes remembers the wonderful team spirit:

'The comradeship was really great, everybody would do anything for anybody. In all the rest of my service I don't think I ever met the same type of people again.'

In mid August 1940 Detling airfield was badly damaged in an air raid. Sixty-seven service and civilian personnel were killed including the Station Commander. Margaret Collins remembers:

'From Loose we could see right across to the North Downs. We could see the planes dive bombing the aerodrome and great pools of black oily smoke rising up. One felt so helpless. There was nothing you could do whilst this dreadful thing was going on.'

The main shelters reserved for the workshop and WAAF personnel had been hit. Corporal Johnny Thompson volunteered to go down into the shelters after the raid:

'First of all we had to try and fight our way through the debris. There were still people alive but I think most of the live ones had already been extricated and all we were doing was to try and drag out some of the bodies. We were ordered to cover the bodies with blankets then they were carried away prior to identification.'

WAAF Corporal Josie Fairclough was awarded the Military Medal for her work on that day. She gave first aid to those wounded in the shelter and remained with the injured until they were taken to hospital. She recalls:

'That was very depressing at the time, especially for the people who were billeted next to those who had died. They had to clear up or had to return the pilots' cars to their parents. That was all terrible but you couldn't dwell on it any more than the pilots themselves could dwell on it, because that would have been self destructive.'

She probably saved many lives, but still remains modest about her efforts today:

'I suppose I went back looking a bit messy and covered in whatever there was and I suppose they thought, "She's been in it she must have done something," but I wasn't aware of having done anything. They made quite a bit of fuss about it and eventually I went up to Buckingham Palace in 1941 and with three other WAAFs was presented to King George VI. It was all a tremendous experience.'

This attitude was typical of the wartime spirit. During the war Martyn Down worked in a voluntary capacity at the West Kent Hospital in Maidstone:

Battle of Britain pilot Jimmy Corbin resplendent in his RAF uniform.
(E. Perriman)

Rosemary Huckerby aged eight framed in a Christmas card to send to her father who was stationed overseas. (R. Huckerby)

'If the stocks of blood and plasma ran out at the hospital I had to be dispatched over to the other side of town and that meant that I had to dash over the bridge to pick up more supplies from the Blood Transfusion Centre in Rocky Hill. Sometimes this happened when a raid was on and I worked up quite a bit of expertise. There's nothing like a bomb coming down to get you off a bike and into the gutter really fast!'

Others remember the worry. Group Captain George Darley from Southborough:

'It was particularly difficult for my wife because we lived in a house quite near dispersal point and we took off there and passed her. She knew what aircraft I flew, therefore it was more of a strain on her. I was rather a busy chap and had plenty to think about. Not everyone came back to the airfield they'd taken off from for the simple reason that you might have to land somewhere else to get some fuel.'

Norman Webber worked in Canterbury during the war as a Message Supervisor for the ARP. The services of the Sea Scouts and Sea Cadets were employed when the telephones were put out of order by an air raid. They took messages between the various ARP posts and the communications centre in Canterbury:

'They were extremely brave, there is no doubt about that. They would come running in with messages when there were planes up overhead and bombs dropping. It was unbelievable. If they had difficulty getting through on their bikes then they got through on foot. Anyhow, they got through somehow.'

Former Luftwaffe pilot Ulrich Steinhilper was shot down and captured near Canterbury in October 1940. He remembers the German position. He feels that Goering pushed his pilots too hard, almost to the point of exhaustion. Unlike Dowding, he did not see any point in taking his pilots away from the front line for a rest. As a result many developed what became known as 'Channel Sickness', as Ulrich describes:

'It was just a funny expression, more or less a nickname, but the way it went some people really got stomach illness with ulcers and other problems. Sometimes when they returned to flying it happened to the same fellows. I too had a high temperature and I couldn't load my guns so we knew "Channel Sickness" was not just physical.'

He continues:

'When I read today the information that the British fighters were gathering by radar, there was no comparison with the German Air Force. When we learned through some secret letters and secret messages that the Spitfire was equipped with a Merlin 3 engine which allowed the Spitfire to climb about 1,000 metres higher, from then on I felt scared.'

Many former RAF pilots claim that in the early days of the Battle of Britain at least, there was little animosity towards the German pilots. It has even been suggested that a degree of respect existed between the two sides but this, as former pilot Stan Walton suggests, was short-lived:

'A camaraderie existed between the RAF and the Luftwaffe from the point of view that if one shot the other down, the one who had been shot down recognised that he had been beaten by a better pilot or a better shot.

'Towards the latter stages of the war that friendship, for want of a better word, just didn't exist. It was a bit cut throat and it was sad. It happened because, let's face it, none of us was trying to kill the men in the planes, we were just trying to knock the plane out of the skies so it couldn't be used again. That is basically what we were after, not killing people.'

As the summer wore on it became increasingly evident that this attitude was not shared by the German pilots. Teenager Martyn Down watched the now frequent dog fights in the skies above Maidstone:

'If a German pilot had to bail out, to the best of my knowledge he was always left to come down in peace and quiet. Unfortunately there were occasions when our pilots had to bail out and the Germans shot them as they descended.'

This account is corroborated by Margaret Collins also from Maidstone:

'Another rather horrid memory is of one of our pilots bailing out and parachuting down and being shot at by a German plane as he dangled there helplessly.'

Ken Geering, a volunteer with the Auxiliary Fire Service, recalls his feelings at the time:

'I was often called to a plane crash, it could be one of ours or one of theirs. If it was one of ours your attitude towards saving life was different, I'm sorry to say. If it was one of theirs an icy feeling came over you. It was nasty. I hated it, looking back on it. You didn't know what you were going to find.'

The British public were only too willing to capture a German pilot and hand him over to the Authorities should the opportunity arise.

Frank Stanford was twelve years old when a German pilot came down at the bottom of his garden in St Margaret's Bay:

'He had blue eyes and fair hair and he came straight towards me. Oh crumbs, he'd got this most wonderful smile on his face. He came up to me and I was very surprised because he spoke a little English and said, "Are your parents at home?" My mother had come out of the house and was shouting at me to come back. He walked up the path with me. I couldn't believe this was the enemy! I can recall him so clearly sitting at the kitchen table having eggs and bacon and a cup of tea, waiting to be taken prisoner. He was really getting tucked in and enjoying this. Whatever they might have been told would happen to them I don't know, but he was very surprised that he was made welcome.

'Then the village bobby turned up on his bike, took off his bicycle clips and had a cup of tea. Then he took some particulars and they got an old van and they took the pilot away. That was the last I saw of him.'

Other pilots who landed in error did not receive such a hospitable welcome. Wilfred Dykes, stationed at Hawkinge, remembers the day a Messerschmitt landed on the runway:

'Three of them came round and we thought they were all going to land. There was firing across the drome and one of them was so low he couldn't get up again so he had to land. The other two made off. He landed close to what was called the old 'Tin Hangar' and jumped out and ran towards those buildings where he was captured and taken to the Guard Room. I think that a lot of people, if they could have got hold of him, would have killed him.'

On 7th September 1940, Hitler switched his bombing offensive to London. By four o'clock in the afternoon the observers based in Kent spotted the first of enemy planes, three hundred bombers escorted by six hundred fighters heading for the Thames estuary. Doug Lee watched the planes pass over Hawkinge:

'They were bombers. They filled the sky, there were so many of them, although they weren't in a real formation. They were scattered loosely all over the sky and I remember making the comment that if they dropped their load now, we've had it.'

Ron Booth from Eltham was playing with his school friends on the afternoon of 7th September. The raids of that day were his first real taste of war:

'I was playing with some school friends of mine about six hundred yards from my home. We had a habit of playing with Dinky toys and soldiers on the path outside and we were so content. I suddenly looked up and the sky which had been so blue and clear had this smoke screen right across in the distance. At the time I didn't take a lot of notice because I thought it might be low cloud. Then I heard this heavy drumming. That was aircraft. I knew it was aircraft engines — not just a few, but hundreds. The smoke screen was coming closer and I started running. The guns started opening up. It sounded as though someone was throwing handfuls of money everywhere, but it was the tinkling of the shrapnel. I still kept running. By the time I reached the house everywhere was hazy with smoke and dust. I was choking. We were safe. There was no glass anywhere, and the curtains were all in tatters. The jagged glass that was left in the windows was tearing the curtains and the blast was taking them in and out.'

Ken Geering, a fire fighter, happened to be in London on that day. He reported to a fire station near Victoria.

'After midnight the German bombers seemed to be cruising around almost at will. There were masses of incendiaries coming down. We were sent to a goods yard in Bishopsgate. We ran out of water. There were no lights and in the end in the middle of the smoke and the muddle, I lost my crew and my pump. Eventually, at about two or three in the morning, I reported back to the station.'

London was bombed for fifty-seven consecutive days and nights and was clearly visible from the middle of Kent as Gladys Townshend in Goudhurst describes:

'You could see all the fires from here burning in London because the searchlights went on in the evenings. It was really remarkable. If it wasn't wartime it would have been wonderful to have been able to see that far, to have seen the searchlights crossing and planes in them and the bullets. But that terrible red glow over London made my blood go cold.'

Biddy Allen from Bilting also remembers watching the Blitz over London:

'The planes mostly came in between Dover and Folkestone. My cocker spaniel could hear the sirens in Dover before I could and she used to go indoors and hide under a piece of furniture. The sky was full of these duck formation bombers, protected by the Messerschmitts, with our Hurricanes and Spitfires roaring in. Overhead you used to get the most colossal battles.

They were heading for London and the ports but we knew the worst times for us would be when the bombers were coming back in a hurry, being chased. Because they couldn't wait to get over the coast. They would unload their bombs on us.'

During the Battle of Britain, children would watch the dog fights taking place in the skies above them with a growing sense of excitement. Geoff Tinley remembers the Hurricane that smashed into the back of a local paper mill:

'I managed to get an elevator trim tab off, as well as some perspex which was very much sought after to make models of things. It was a new plastic, we'd never seen things of that sort before. You were always trying to get there before the Police or the Military arrived to put a guard on it. Those who could get the most attractive souvenirs were King for the day, so to speak. Pieces of shrapnel were very collectable items and I can remember one piece that was just about as heavy as one could carry. That was a German shell and I was the envy of our gang for quite a while with this massive piece. It all collected in the back garden and slowly accumulated rust. One or two pieces were prized souvenirs, particularly pieces of German aircraft.'

Collecting souvenirs of the war became a popular past-time for many children. Ian Moat was more enterprising than most:

'At one time my brother and I put on an exhibition and charged the neighbours three pence (1½p) a time, to see our exhibits.'

This passion for collecting memorabilia landed many children into trouble, both with the authorities and with their parents. The antics of Gladys Town-shend's two boys, particularly the eldest one Derek who was then ten years old, gave her a few nasty surprises:

'We had all sorts of regiments of soldiers around here and naturally one of them must have given him a big empty shell about eighteen inches long. He knew I wouldn't allow him to have it indoors so he buried it in the garden. He went to school and I thought I'd do some gardening and I unearthed this bit of shrapnel.

'I was really panic stricken! I called the guard on duty and said I'd got this bullet in my garden and he came and got it out and laughed like mad. Another day I was clearing up their bedroom and I thought I'd see what was in one of the big drawers. It was a bit hard to pull at first, it stuck a bit. When I got it open it was completely full of German and English shells of all descriptions. My brother-in-law happened to call at the time and he took them away and threw them into the local pond.'

As the war progressed many children were forced to witness scenes that even adults found difficult to accept. As a result the childhood of many wartime children ended before it ever really began. This was true of Barbra Letchford who, as a young girl in 1940, failed to appreciate what war really meant:

'We used to have a corny quirk. When we were walking home from school we used to say to one another, "See you in the morning if we're not all dead". We thought that was funny. As an adult that just seems sick.'

Her naïvety was short-lived:

'We used to sleep down in the shelters some nights and we would hear the noise of the aircraft and the guns. I was very frightened. I used to put my hands on my ears to shut out the noise and ask the Almighty to "please make them go away"! Then one evening we were indoors wondering whether to nip out down the shelter because the guns had already started firing when a German bomber got caught in the searchlights. I suddenly remember feeling sorry for him.'

A certain wartime language evolved as Martyn Down recalls:

'People who had previously talked to you about the weather would now say, "They are catching it over West Malling," or "Gosh, I can see they are catching it over Chatham."'

Doug Lee remembers another curious phrase:

'I would listen to the pilots talking and hear how they would say they had caught the Germans "with their trousers down". This meant they had got the bombers without their fighter escort.'

There were conflicting views on Hilter's intention in launching the raids. Maidstone bridge was always considered vulnerable, not only because it crossed the River Medway but also because of the major industries which surrounded it. Martyn Down remembers that:

'The Maidstone housewife could see that the object of the exercise was to knock out the bridge and therefore knock out the electricity works, the gas works, and thus put paid to our Sunday lunches. Another aspect occurred to thinking drinkers in the pubs and clubs who could see that if they knocked out Fremlins, Style & Winch and Mason's Breweries this was going to be a severe psychological blow. Between the Stukas and seeing our Sunday lunches and our beer supplies go down it was quite clearly a psychological warfare starting up straight away. Even the smaller fry could see that if Sharps Toffee Works and Foster Clarks Custard Factory were hit, the end of the world really was nigh!'

Although communal shelters had been provided at regular intervals in all towns, many people in Kent sought safety in the tunnels which ran under the cliffs in Ramsgate and Dover. Often the air raid warning sounded too late and there was no time to get to the shelter. People would then hide wherever they could and little thought about the consequences of their actions. Wilfred Dykes explains:

151

'At one time on the dispersal we had marquees and, silly as it may seem, we ran into a marquee during a raid because you thought you were out of sight! Another time I remember running into the petrol dump. I knew it was quite well reinforced but actually one of the pilots followed me and said "This is a lovely place to be." I said, "Yes, there's only thousands of gallons of petrol in here." I'm afraid he went out quick.'

Tom Miller, a fruit farmer, remembers picking blackcurrants during the Battle of Britain at Eastry:

'We had a canvas hut. It was a home-made affair, with some hurdles covered in tarpaulin which I'd put up to keep the blackcurrants and the boxes dry in case it rained. When the siren went everybody rushed under this tarpaulin. You felt as if you were somehow safe if you had your head under something.'

Charlie Wheeler remembers being called to Lyminge one day:

'That put a shiver right up our backs because being out in the open we knew what it would be like. As three bombers came over in the afternoon we all lay underneath a lorry and when we came out I had to laugh! Nearly all of us had our head and shoulders covered underneath the lorry but our behinds and legs were sticking out.'

Josie Fairclough recalls the efforts people went to to make life more bearable in the shelters during the Battle of Britain:

'We used to do quiz games and tell stories. Sometimes people used to sing and anyone who had a mouth organ was very popular. The most frustrating part about it was that when the siren went you had to throw down whatever you were doing and just leave it and all that time was wasted. If you'd left something cooking, it was probably burnt.'

Biddy Allen agrees with Josie: 'The raids always seemed to happen at meal times. I rather think that was deliberate.'

Gordon Farrer, a native of Tunbridge Wells, was stationed at Gibraltar Farm. The farm was a few miles outside Chatham and possessed a small battery of guns:

'In September during the Battle of Britain, I had a twelve-hour Pass and decided to drive to Tunbridge Wells and collect my father. We were going to drive to the Nevill Golf Club for a few holes of golf.
'At the precise moment of entering the Club Car Park a Ju88, Germany's latest and most successful twin-engined bomber at that time, came out of a cloud and dropped a stick of bombs. Fortunately they all missed the Club House and landed on the 18th fairway in front of the Car Park and the Club House.
'On entering the Members Lounge, despite this somewhat terrifying experience, I was rather amused to find at least 10 members crammed

under the bar billiards table in the corner for cover. As the course was very wet the bombs had gone in fairly deep, but they threw up the most incredible amount of mud all over the front of the Club House. The two leading rows of cars in the car park facing the 18th fairway were literally unrecognisable.

'Finally, with typical British aplomb, we went out and played twelve holes of golf. Apart from having to clear hundreds of cartridge and cannon shell cases off the Greens before we could putt, we had a most enjoyable game!'

In a speech broadcast to the nation on 11th September 1940, Winston Churchill warned the people of Britain that a heavy full scale invasion of this island was being prepared with all the usual German thoroughness and method.

Ack-Ack Operator Laurie Springett, based at Dover, was prepared to fight this invasion to the death:

'We were to fight to the finish. If for any reason we did get overrun we were to go down into Dover, if possible, and join the Infantry in the street fighting. Our site had several hundred telephone poles made of wood, all around it. This meant you couldn't land a glider without hitting something.'

In order to make an invasion as difficult as possible, rolls of barbed wire were placed on the beaches. Road blocks consisting of iron posts just wide enough to let a bus through were also erected. Sign posts and milestones were removed. Everything possible was done to ensure that, should an invasion take place, the Germans would find their path strewn with obstacles.

14th September dawned cloudy with a number of thunder storms over the South East of England. Pilots and civilians alike prayed for days like this, particularly at this crucial stage of the battle, because it meant that there was less likelihood of a raid. The pilots still had to remain on standby but tried to relax in between trying to snatch some sleep. Many pilots socialised with their ground crew or other members back at base as Wilfred Dykes recalls:

'Sometimes when they hadn't been scrambled or were waiting to scramble, we would play football and generally have a joke.'

Many found it difficult to unwind until they were officially classed as 'off duty'. Former pilot Stan Walton:

'If we had to stay on Station because we were on Standby, we'd play snooker or table tennis or once again just sit around snoozing. Off duty of course we went to dances and down to the pub. You were very good at drinking pints if you were a pilot.'

Coastal gunner Harry Eede discovered a lack of female companionship somewhat hampered his social life. Harry and his friend arranged dances at the Pavilion in Folkestone every Tuesday night:

'At first we couldn't get the girls here because there was no transport. When you walk from here to the Pavilion you have to walk along the cliff tops and a plane would suddenly sneak in and machine gun anything moving, so they were very nervous of that. So we couldn't get the girls. We took a chance and hired a double-decker East Kent bus and stood it outside 'Debenhams', which was Bobby's in those days, and put a Bombardier in charge of it. He shouted out, "Girls only for the dance". No men were allowed to get aboard as we had all the men we wanted. The girls patronised it, and came down in their droves. It was the only dance around for miles as people couldn't run functions like that normally. I was lucky, I met my wife there.'

However, even off-duty it was impossible to relax, as Wilfred Dykes recalls:

'I went down to the cinema in Folkestone with my wife. Suddenly a message came up on the screen: "Ack-Ack battery report back. So and so troops report back!" Then it was "All troops return immediately to barrracks." We realised then that something was really in the air.'

Many of those who took part in the Battle of Britain were not British by birth. Wing Commander George Kellett of Benenden helped to form 303 Polish Squadron, which was based at Northolt. It was not the easiest of tasks:

'They may have been a bit frightened and they certainly were not a very happy fraternity. They didn't like their own officers. I don't say they were difficult to deal with, because they were very loyal, but at the same time their politics were obviously a great problem. Some of them were Feudal and some of them were Communists and so it went on. Some could speak a little French, some quite a bit of French, some not a word. We had to translate all books on maintenance, on armaments, on everything, into Polish so that they could understand them. That was a big enough problem. They all had to be taught to fly Hurricanes, as they'd never flown an aircraft with a retractable undercarriage before.'

It was also the Polish pilots who caused their fair share of problems amongst the civilian population in Kent. Eastchurch became the recognised aerodrome for members of the Polish Airforce until May 1940. At the time many of the locals complained that they upset the peace of the English countryside, driving cars too fast down the lanes and spending too much of their spare time in dubious female company. For all that the Polish pilots became universally popular. They were said by many to be the bravest of all, as Peter Matthews of Number One Squadron recalls:

'They were very keen to beat the Germans and they really felt very strongly about them. They had such a terrible time in Poland they felt that the only decent German was a dead German and they worked that way.'

In the lead-up to the Battle of Britain, German High Command failed to appreciate how important Radar had become to the RAF as a means of detecting the build up of enemy aircraft. Radar acted as an early warning system, giving prior warning of a forthcoming raid. From this it was possible to deduce vital information about the strength, altitude and direction of flight of the enemy aircraft. However, the term 'Radar' was not coined until 1943. Until then it was known as RDF or 'Radio Direction Finding'. Its development was gradual.

In 1935 a series of detection stations known as 'Chain Home Stations' were established all around the coast between Southampton and the Tyne. There were two in Kent located at Dunkirk and Dover. The disadvantage of CH stations was that they failed to detect aircraft that flew below a certain height, so in 1939 a second series of Chain Home Low Stations were built. Within the year this system was able to detect the formation of enemy bombers over the French coast. The Hurricanes and Spitfires of Fighter Command were in the air to meet them by the time they got to Kent. The disadvantage of this system was that British radar chains were only capable of looking out to sea. Once the bombers crossed the English coastline the Observer Corps provided the sole means of tracing the path taken by the enemy. This information provided by RDF and the men of the Observer Corps was eventually passed on to the pilots by the Radio Operator in the sector operations room.

The information provided by Radar was also to prove useful to night fighter crews. Early experiments using Radar equipped aircraft were carried out at Manston shortly after war was declared. The pilot and his Radar Operator would take off in a Blenheim bomber with various pieces of equipment, including radio boxes and Cathode Ray Tubes. Each aircraft became a little Radar Station in itself, sending out and supposedly receiving information back about the location of enemy aircraft. These experiments were not always successful, as Wing Commander Norman Hayes remembers. Eventually, however, RDF was to become one of the RAF's most valuable assets:

'My first experience with this equipment was a disaster. Once we were up, the Radar Operator switched on the gear. There was a terrible smell of burning and rather a lot of smoke. We had to switch if off again.'

15th September 1940 was the most decisive day of the Battle of Britain. By late morning Radar showed large formations of enemy squadrons assembling in the skies above Calais and Bolougne. Many of the pilots who took part in the battle on that epic day showed tremendous bravery and determination. Pilot Jimmy Corbin was travelling by car between Essex and RAF Kenley on 15th September:

'I arrived at Kenley. We drove to the dispersal point where a Squadron had just landed after an Operation. I remember seeing some young Pilot Officer who had a bullet through his perspex hood. He was calming picking out the bits of perspex from his face, which was covered in blood. I thought, "This is a good start."'

In the Nine O'Clock news bulletin that evening the BBC announced that 183 enemy planes has been shot down. The figures were exaggerated but the announcement was a tremendous morale booster. WAAF Josie Fairclough was based at Detling during the Battle of Britain:

'You used to listen to the news and hear how many had been brought down. Everyone crowded in to say, "What's the score?" When we heard, we all bounced back and thought we'd got on top of the Germans.'

Despite the battle taking place in the skies overhead, the hop-picking season went ahead as usual that year. Frank Bond of Goudhurst, who was a farm worker at the time, remembers the initial reluctance of the Londoners to come to Kent in September 1940:

'In 1940 it was the bombing of London that picked the hops. Prior to the bombing, the Londoners thought they were in a better position than we were in Kent. Once the Germans started bombing London they came down alright and I don't think they were eager to go home. Some of them took a bit of persuading to go back up there.'

Ruth Wilson of Faversham agrees:

'When London was badly bombed they came out of their shelters to find their house had gone or had been badly damaged. They then jumped on any available vehicle coming down to the Kent hop fields. Some of them were dressed only in nightdresses and slippers. Others were pregnant. They even brought their animals with them. My father told me to drop everything and report to the food office.

'From the food office we went to the hop fields where we issued emergency cards for milk for the babies and food. It was quite a difficult task because you'd be interviewing someone and if an aeroplane came over they would just disappear into the bines. When the time came to go home they refused to go back to London. The hop huts where they had been living provided only temporary accommodation, so my father had to arrange to move all these Londoners to another part of the country.'

Mary Wickham of Combourne Farm, Goudhurst, had problems getting the hops picked in 1940:

'It was in 1940 that the Londoners thought we were going to have fights and things. Well, we were having quite a bit of trouble until London was bombed and then they all came down in a rush. They thought they'd be out of harm's way here. There were no bombs falling all over them here and nobody got hurt. We expected about three hundred families. When we were short of pickers we took the hops up to the cottages in the village. They had a bin outside their doors and we went and measured them out at night. Near the pond in the village we also had a bin. Anyone who liked could go and pick the hops and the money went to the Spitfire Fund.'

Others who had connections with the county through many years of hop picking decided that it would be safer if they could find a way of moving out of London permanently. Lilian Blow and her husband Albert managed to move down in the autumn of 1939, but this was not easy:

'We wanted to get out of London because of the babies and it was quite alright for a time. We came down as soon as the baby was old enough to be christened, and lived with our relations. The farmer was good enough to find my husband a job, but the following spring I was expected to go out to work which I'd never done before being a town girl. I had to do hop trailing, which was all foreign to me. But there you are, I had a go! I had to take two babies and a pram and pull them across fields. It was really hard work and it continued throughout summer fruit picking and hop picking. At hopping I earned 6d (2½p) the first day. Heart breaking that was. You'd come home, see to the babies, cook our meal which was on an open fire range, get them to bed, do my housework and get a meal partly cooked for the next day otherwise we wouldn't have got one. It was really hard work, all the time. I never knew what it was to work on the land.'

However, her husband Albert comments that by the end of the war they had got their own cottage, and he had managed to get a good job.

Many hop pickers saw their fair share of incidents in the Battle of Britain, as Michael Fitzgerald remembers:

'1940, that's when it started. I remember one Sunday morning coming back from the local pub, The Red Cow. Ten men all walking along the lane talking and joking. Suddenly the siren sounded. We took no notice and carried on walking. Just as we got to the farm we saw the Germans going over, swarms of them all in formation. Then we heard the bombs coming down, so we quickly dived into the ditch. I stood up and saw a string of bombs go straight across the farm. We ran down to the huts where the women and kids were. They were crying and screaming, all huddled in the huts. Thank God nobody got hurt.

'The first bomb dropped in the orchard which was fifty yards away and the next one was in the hop field which was just beyond that. That was an unexploded bomb which had sliced through the soil like butter. My brother-in-law and I went to look at it. Little did we know that we could have been blown to pieces then and there. Two bins were blown up in the air. Good job it wasn't a week day or there would have been several people injured. We ran back to the huts and the police were telling us we'd have to be evacuated to Church Farm up the road. When we got there there was nowhere to sleep as their hop pickers were in the huts, so they put us in a black barn and some cow sheds. There were no cows there of course, but the conditions were terrible!

'We finished picking the hops at Church Farm then decided we could continue picking back at our farm. The unexploded bombs were still in the fields but we walked backwards and forwards to finish the hops.'

However, life in the towns was equally hard, particularly when it came to organising social gatherings, as Bobbie Stacey explains:

'They just shut down any gatherings in the town. You weren't allowed to gather together anywhere except for church services. That was the only gathering that was allowed at all. So there was nothing to do. My father and mother, who had been in the Operatic Society and in the Choral Union, suddenly thought, "We must sing," so they sent out a rather amusing letter to a whole lot of friends who also sang. They came whenever they could and we all sang. Eventually we managed to get the ex-borough organist to really give us a good going-over and we formed quite a big choir called the Dover Singers.'

Hop pickers in Kent were in constant danger during the Battle of Britain. Many farmers dug trenches for their workers to take shelter. Peggie Jenkins was with a school party who had been asked to help with hop picking. However, the day did not go according to plan:

'We spent ten minutes picking hops and the rest of the day we spent in a ditch with gas masks floating up and down on the river. We were terrified because there were dog fights over the top of us and machine gunning all the time. In the end, when it all died down, the teacher said, "I can't stand this, we're all going home." So we piled into the lorries and went back.'

Many people built shelters in their gardens in the weeks before war was declared. Others waited until the air raids started and often regretted their decision.

Winifred Baker of St Mary's Platt recalls testing out her shelter:

'It was only when the Blitz started that we had a shelter dug. It was done by a Maidstone firm and it was very strong. The first night it was finished my parents were with me and I suggested that we slept down there. We put a double mattress down. It was just four foot six inches long and four of us slept down there. It was the most dreadful night as nobody could stretch out. Then we were disturbed in the middle of the night by the person who had promised to shut my chickens up creeping around. My father thought the Germans had come and that was that.'

Doris Ayres of Maidstone recalls that many of her pupils hated going down to the shelters:

'They called them trenches but they were really tunnels about a yard under the earth, tunnelled in a zig-zag pattern so that if a bomb dropped one end it couldn't get to the other. The girls would train to rush to these shelters but by the time things got a bit busy in the Battle of Britain they were quite indifferent to danger. Sometimes we had to rush up the drive and fetch them down if they were going into the school in the morning and there was a raid. They didn't want to go down the trenches.'

Although the RAF failed to realise it at the time, the Battle of Britain was effectively over by mid-September. 'Operation Sealion', the German invasion of the British Isles, had been abandoned. The Luftwaffe had failed to gain air supremacy. Nevertheless the precautions adopted to thwart a possible invasion remained in force. A twenty mile area inland from the South coast, which extended from The Wash to Rye in Sussex, was declared a Defence area. Nobody could visit that part of the country without good reason, as Jeannie Blackmore remembers:

> 'If we were going towards the coast from Canterbury in the direction of Dover or Folkestone, the bus would be stopped at a certain area well outside the city. In the case of Dover it was Temple Ewell. A policeman or a member of military personnel would board the bus and you would have to show your identity card. You would also have to state your reasons for wanting to visit the town.'

The second Christmas of the war was a fairly bleak time, as Evelyn Wilson remembers:

> 'Ordnance Street, next to Chatham Railway Station, had been badly bombed before Christmas. The Germans were trying to get to the station. My mum had a friend who lived up there and we went to visit her. When we got there all the paperchains were floating in the roadway. It was very sad seeing all that.'

Jeanne Blackwell recalls the loneliness of that Christmas:

> 'In the main I think most of the men were away. If your men were home you were lucky. I think Christmas just disappeared really.'

1940 had been a grim year for those living in the County of Kent. Ken Geering recalls his feelings as the year drew to a close:

> 'The war didn't stop for Christmas Day or Boxing Day. The war went on all the time. It was a seven day a week job.'

MERESBOROUGH BOOKS

17 Station Road, Rainham, Kent. ME8 7RS

Medway (0634) 388812   Fax Medway (0634) 378501

We are a specialist publisher of books about Kent. Our books are available in bookshops throughout the county, including our own large shop at this address. If ordering by post please add 10% towards p&p (minimum 30p, orders over £25 post free). Our publications include:

TARGET FOLKESTONE by Roy Humphreys

192 pages, 125 illustrations. Paperback £7.95.

A day by day record of a town at war compiled from thorough researches in the official records blended with personal memories of many citizens of Folkestone.

AIRCRAFT CASUALTIES IN KENT. Part 1: 1939 to 1940
Compiled by G.G. Baxter, K.A. Owen and P. Baldock
of the Kent Aviation Research Society

128 pages. Hardback £12.95

A detailed listing of 1,497 aircraft crashes in the county in this period, giving details of the aircraft and personnel involved.

KENT'S OWN by Robin J. Brooks

The history of 500 (County of Kent) Squadron of the RAAF. Hardback £5.95.

FROM MOTHS TO MERLINS by Robin J. Brooks

The history of West Malling Airfield. Paperback £4.95.

THE BLITZ OF CANTERBURY by Paul Crampton

A pictorial record of the city at war. Large format paperback £3.50.

PRELUDE TO WAR: Aviation in Kent 1938-39

A series of articles by members of the Kent Aviation Historical Research Society. Paperback £2.50.

TROOPSHIPS TO CALAIS by Derek Spiers

The story of Calais as a military port from 1944 to 1947 and the ships which served it, mostly from Dover and Folkestone. Hardback £11.95.

BYGONE KENT. A monthly magazine on all aspects of Kent history founded in 1979. £1.50 per month from bookshops and newsagents or £16.50 by post (£24.00 overseas) for 12 issues (1991 prices).